Conversations with
Lord Byron on Perversion,
163 Years after
His Lordship's Death

Books by Amanda Prantera

AMANDA PRANTERA

Conversations with
Lord Byron on Perversion,
163 Years after
His Lordship's Death

New York Atheneum *1987*

Atheneum
Macmillan Publishing Company
866 Third Avenue, New York, N.Y. 10022

Library of Congress Cataloging-in-Publication Data
Prantera, Amanda.
Conversations with Lord Byron on perversion,
163 years after His Lordship's death.
1. Byron, George Gordon Byron, Baron, 1788–1824,
in fiction, drama, poetry, etc.   I. Title.
PR6066.R325.C6   1987   821'.7   87-17354
ISBN 0-689-11882-1

10 9 8 7 6 5 4 3 2 1

Printed in the United States of America

To Alexander

'In Ja und Nein bestehen alle Dinge.'
J. Boehme

1 'The Hardware'

The room made a curious headquarters for a pioneer experiment in Artificial Intelligence. There were no white-coated technicians to be seen in it, no panels flashing with lights or buzzing with buzzers, no shiny metal surfaces — apart that is from the lid of a silver cigar box — and very little even in the way of desks. True, there were books enough, and files and papers and so forth scattered around — proving, or at least suggesting, that some kind of intellectual activity was going on; but since most of these were stacked in a wobbly, higgledy-piggledy fashion, as often as not with an overflowing ashtray on top of the pile, or a packet of toffees, an apple-core or somebody's cardigan, they didn't go far towards creating the kind of atmosphere one would somehow have expected. The chief furnishings, computer apart, consisted of a couple of baggy armchairs, a fireplace full of dusty fircones, a low coffee table set before it, heavily charged with ornaments, vases of flowers and yet more books, a furry mat, which looked as if it had been primarily designed for lending camouflage to spaniels, and a grubby, beige velvet sofa almost as wide and rumpled as a bed. It was the sort of comfortable, early nineteenth-century-flavoured room in which the subject of the experiment himself would have looked more at home than did a computer; although this particular computer, being

9

beige and grubby like the sofa and no thicker or noisier than a sewing machine, in point of fact fitted in with the rest quite well.

Three people normally worked in the room. Two of them were assistants to the Professor in charge of the experiment (and the brain behind it, although on his own admission, quite far behind it by now), while the third was a research student of Romantic literature — younger than the others and often referred to by them with a faint groan as if the species were one they were familiar with to their cost, as 'the Byron expert'. The Professor himself was seldom to be seen there. He had long since set up his own independent headquarters in the pantry downstairs — a place from which he emerged rarely, either to conduct long, plaintive, transatlantic calls from a telephone in the passageway, or else to mutter irritably to whoever happened to be passing about the difficulties he was having in raking in sufficient grants for them to carry on. Recently, though, having just received a large cheque from the honorary secretary of an organization called the ULBL — the Universal League of Byron Lovers (of which category, by the way, there seemed to be as many members, if not more, than there were when his Lordship was alive to reciprocate their affection) — funds had been of less worry to him, and he had taken to climbing the stairs more often and to popping his head round the door in order to keep an eye on what he called his 'Brainchild Harold' in its final phase.

It was a significant phase. That much at least could be seen from the smouldering ashtrays and litter of discarded toffee papers and from the increased number and pace of the Professor's sorties from the pantry, but you could also tell from the face of the three lesser ministers as they hovered over the terminal and from the jerky, shrill way they spoke to one another, that something exciting or at any rate argument-worthy was going on.

Their voices could be heard cutting across each others', pitch rather than loudness being the chosen way of cutting. 'The fatness,' the Byron expert was saying, at the top of her register. 'Fancy it asking whether it was fat! And the business about his sister. That was extraordinary wasn't it, don't you think? And when it said, "Umph!" And when it asked what had happened to Tita, the gondolier? And that bit about the Greek government? And when it wanted to know the whereabouts of the Elgin Marbles, and the Newfoundland dog, and how the will had been executed and things, and . . . ?'

'I think you're missing the point,' the female assistant interrupted her. 'The really extraordinary thing as far as I'm concerned is it's bending back on itself and trying to modify the data. When it got hold of Trelawny's comment about both the legs of Byron's corpse being withered like a satyr's, and said it was a damned lie. Or yesterday when it corrected that word in one of the letters. That's the real advance — the real breakthrough.'

'Not necessarily,' piped up the other — a thin, fish-like man in his early thirties. 'I think you are missing the point too. The Trelawny episode may have looked a bit freakish, OK, but the reply is a stock one that it's often used before when it got huffy. And as to the word, well it's got both definitions in its dictionary, after all. There's no reason why it shouldn't note the discrepancy and try to iron it out. I mean when he said that running into debt was "epidemic" in his family, Byron himself probably *did* mean "endemic". It was a slip of the pen. Or else he just got into a muddle with

11

his terms. A good program *should* correct a thing like that. It's nothing to get excited about.'

'Ho, ho. Isn't it? What if it starts wanting to re-write some of the poems then? What then?'

The fish-like man laughed.

'What if it comes up with a *new* poem?' put in the Byron expert quickly, a slight tremor in her voice as she got to the 'new'.

The man gave a skip, landing deftly on his rubber-soled shoes. 'Fair question,' he said. The fairness of it evidently surprised him. 'Well, I suppose it *can* of course. There's a Bach program that can trot out fugues for you, as you've probably heard. In theory there's no reason why ours shouldn't do the same in its own field. It's got enough schematic data, and it's got the words. The question though is: not so much can it but *will* it? Will it *feel* like it, I mean' — and he gave an ironic little bow towards his colleague — 'now that all these moodiness parameters have been inserted. Or will it bog itself down in its own spleen?'

There was a moment's silence during which the two assistants looked hard at one another across some deep theoretical divide. The man was the first to lower his eyes.

'Anyway, don't bother your head with things like that, Anna,' he went on to the researcher, his voice still heavy with irony but quieter now that it had no others to contend with, 'if it does it'll probably open up a whole new chapter in computer science, and I'll have to eat my hat and a lot more besides — but that's our affair; the thing for you to work on now is this inference it has come up with about the mysterious Thyrza of the poems. Joking apart, this is round about the most interesting thing we've hit on so far. A program — even a program as rich as this — obviously

12

can't tell us anything new about his Lordship, but it can tell us something different. Something that even the most conscientious of his biographers may have overlooked. That's the real point.' And shifting his feet into a senatorial stance he declaimed loudly with a lifted forefinger: 'So — was the famous "Thyrza" a man after all, when for the past two hundred years everyone has always assumed she was a woman?'

The researcher coughed. 'The other way round,' she corrected him, 'Thyrza is generally thought to have been a man — a choirboy, as a matter of fact.'

'Oh well, then,' he continued, still waving the fore-finger but a little more archly, 'put it this way: was Britain's most renowned womanizer just another of our island's fairies? There's the hunting ground for you. That's the question you must concentrate on now.'

'Well, it's a bit more complex than that,' the girl objected; 'I don't think we'll get much of an answer if we set about it in those terms, knowing how touchy the program gets about things like that. Still . . .' and she glanced through a sheaf of papers lying at her elbow, 'it did handle the "Ape" rather neatly, didn't it? I loved it when it did that. Of course it mightn't have been a new answer exactly — I'll have to check and see if someone else has ever suggested it before — but I thought it was pretty impressive.'

'What was that about the Ape?' asked the woman assistant, turning sharply. 'I must have missed that bit.'

The girl smiled, evidently pleased to be on the explaining side for a change. 'Oh, it's a famous old controversy. There's a passage in one of Byron's letters to his confidante, Lady Melbourne, where he mentions the birth of his sister's latest child, and says, "It is *not* an Ape, and if it is, it will be my fault." Commentators have often thought this shows he was worried about the child being deformed.'

'Aha,' said the assistant. 'Because it was *his* child, you mean, the naughty fellow? Incest. Inbreeding. And the sins of the fathers.'

'Yes, that's right. Only others say the child couldn't have been Byron's or he'd have taken more interest in it later on. He was always a fairly affectionate father, you see, in his offhand way. A lot of arguing has always gone on about it.'

The assistant glanced at her watch and gave a little tap on the glass.

'Well?' she prompted.

'Well, I asked the program about it last night, and do you know what it said? It said that "Ape" was a private word used by the Melbournes and their circle to refer to the besotted young ladies who went into swoons over Byron at parties and things when he was all the rage. A fan. A what do you call it? A devotee. So when he wrote it in the letter, so the program said, he wasn't talking about the child at all, but about his sister; and what he meant was that his sister wasn't besotted about him in that way at all, and that if she did become so it would be his fault, not hers. Look, it's here somewhere on the print-out.' And she consulted a long muddle of paper on the floor, reading off from it in a high, clear voice: 'THE TERM "APE" REFERS TO MY SISTER, AUGUSTA. HER ADMIRATION FOR ME WAS NEITHER FOOLISH NOR BLIND. SHE WAS, I.E., NO APE. LADY MELBOURNE WAS ANXIOUS ABOUT THE CONSEQUENCES OF OUR STRONG FEELINGS FOR ONE ANOTHER AT THAT TIME, AND MY LETTER OF APRIL 25TH, 1814 WAS WRITTEN TO ASSURE HER THAT HER FEARS WERE GROUNDLESS ON AUGUSTA'S BEHALF.' She turned to the assistant with a nod of satisfaction. 'Now, what do you think of that?'

The woman frowned. 'Mmm. Not bad at all. How did it back it up, though?'

'Mostly quotes from letters, I think,' said the girl, consulting her notes. 'Lady Melbourne's nieces, for example, seem to use it quite often: so-and-so is a downright "Ape"; Caro was "apish" this evening; and so on. And one of them — Annabella Milbanke, the one that marries Byron in the end — even puts it in a poem. Here we are; I took a photocopy of it. The title is "Byromania" and it ends up with: "Then grant me, Jove, to wear some other shape, and be an anything except an Ape." '

The woman sniffed. 'If that was what it meant, then she did become one seeing that she married him,' she commented drily.

'I suppose she did,' agreed the researcher, 'in a very staid way. But anyway it was a good bit of detective work on the program's part, don't you think?'

The assistant bit on a long, pearly fingernail and spat it elegantly in the air. 'Oh yes indeed,' she agreed. 'It's one in the eye for the Professor at any rate. He didn't seem to think the program would be able to do research work at all with the latest innovations we've given it. To my way of thinking, though, as a performance it's a bit tame. You others can say what you like, but *I* still think that the star turn to date is the unmasking of Trelawny.'

The researcher looked down and said quietly, 'And *I* still think it is the fatness.'

The male assistant exchanged glances with his colleague and sighed. 'Forget the fatness, Anna, and stick to the "Thyrza" question for today, there's a good girl,' he said, giving a tap on the researcher's shoulder. 'Keep the print-outs separate, especially if you switch to "output only" during lunch break, and we'll go over them this evening and see if we can't clear his Lordship of the charges against his manhood. No fatness; just poetry and sex. And remember it's the language you want to watch out for all the time. OK?'

The girl went back to her tapping at the keyboard. 'OK,' she agreed, 'only it isn't me who keeps bringing up the subject.' And with a quick glance into the screen to make sure that the assistants had gone back to their own work and were no longer watching over her shoulder, she gave a guilty wriggle on the chair and typed swiftly: PLEASE NOT TO WORRY SO. YOUR LORDSHIP IS BEAUTIFULLY THIN.

Of course, like so many people who are relatively unfamiliar with computers, she was probably amongst other things committing the error of confusing software with hardware; but if so, what she wrote was perfectly true: the computer, as we have seen, was a narrow one. The program, on the other hand, was wide.

2 'The Software'

A word about the program before we go on to watch it at work. The LB program (LB, naturally, standing as elsewhere for Lord Byron) was a variation of what is nowadays called an 'expert system', the variation being that it was — as most of us are supposed to be in our more boring ways — an expert about itself. Into it had been fed, in codified form, every detail and every snippet of information that was available about the poet's life and works: where Byron was on March the whatsit in the year x, what he ate for dinner on that day (assuming that he or anyone else recorded it), what he was feeling like, who he met, who he wrote to and what he wrote; what Byron thought of Shelley; what he thought Shelley thought of him; what he thought Mrs Shelley thought of him and vice versa; what he thought of Mrs Shelley's step-sister (i.e. that she was a 'damned bitch'), and so on and so forth; but not what *Shelley* thought of Mrs Shelley's step-sister, of course, unless Byron happened to have been told this by Shelley first hand, or there was some other way in which he could have found it out. For although the program *did* store a number of related facts unknown to Byron, and a good deal on episodes which took place after his death, the data were kept separate and the access to them differentiated, so as to prevent the hindsight that they gave from infecting the authentic reminiscences. In short, it

17

contained just about everything pertinent to Byron's very personal life-history that has come down to us; and since he was such a frank and voluble correspondent, and had so many articulate friends and diligent chroniclers, this in fact was quite a lot and went to make up a very full and well-stocked program.

Rumour had it, although perhaps with a pinch of exaggeration, that as many as two hundred students of literature in England and America were employed in the earlier stages for the business of the codifying — exaggerated or not, it was an idea that Byron himself would probably have found appealing, having always been very keen on building up his reputation on the far side of the Atlantic.

Besides being full, it was also very flexible. It had — again as most of us are presumed to have, although opinions vary as to the exact number — a three-level memory. A deep memory for the long-term storage of data, a surface memory for the handling of whatever the current topic of discourse happened to be, and a sort of interim memory between the two, where things could float up to the top or sift down to the bottom again, depending on the interest value of the pieces of information in question.

'Interest', of course, even between a pair of cautionary quote marks, may sound a bit out of place when speaking of nothing more subtle than a machine with off and on switches inside it, but all it boiled down to really was that certain topics — certain symbols, that is, and their equivalent explanations — had been given a numbered rating, from 1 to 8 or thereabouts, which directed, or influenced anyway, the program's choice of answer. Marriage, for example, separation, poor Lady Byron herself, the names of hostile literary critics — things like these had been given a pretty high 'interest' rating (and a high 'irritability' rating too), because Byron the man had tended to get worked up about them when alive. Whereas a mention of physical beauty, or animals, or the writings of Rousseau (all things that he had liked), or the name of anyone of whom he had been particularly fond, while it might have the same rating of interest, would have a high charge of 'sympathy' also to distinguish it from the other kind. Mathematics, at the opposite end of the scale, topped the bill in 'boredom' by having no interest value whatever. You could almost hear the computer yawn whenever it was mentioned. Similarly politics, which, unless stirring topics such as liberty or tyrannicide were touched on, usually generated a set reply, like 'Is that so?', or 'Indeed?', or 'I really am no judge of these things.' Homosexuality tended to affect the program negatively too, although in a slightly different way, having been allotted a medium 'interest' but a high 'anxiety' tax, and when the subject was brought up the machine would first rattle itself into a state and then, like as not, switch itself off entirely and refuse to budge for quite some minutes. Money got it into a twist, too, sometimes. Religion on the other hand tended to produce flippant replies, unless introduced from a position of previous seriousness on the program's part when it could on occasion lead to ponderous and surprisingly long-winded ones. And to take a still more complex case, someone like Madame de Staël had ratings which varied according to the date, seeing that Byron disliked her sharply to begin with, then found her simply a bit of a pill, and then, very slowly, came round to liking her a good deal.

This, anyway, was the gist of the device, and although it may sound sophisticated to those who are strangers to the field (the exact name for which is not so much Artificial Intelligence, by the way, as Cognitive Emulation), by insiders' standards it was fairly crude and not a little controversial. As we have seen, the assistant of the fish-face had no patience with it at all; the Professor himself took a neutral stand, as he did on most things; while his second assistant, who was responsible for its inclusion (although she didn't actually think up the mechanics of it for herself, but borrowed them from the work of others), championed it fiercely. The program was more like a real brain this way, she insisted; without the parameters to guide it, it would have been quite unable to link up topics of its own accord the way it did, but would just have had to comb its way exhaustively through its thesaurus in search of synonyms.

She may have been right. However awkward at times, the program's moodiness did in fact seem to make it flit about with a certain sense of direction and a certain economy. Although crude or refined, useful or not, from the operator's point of view it was definitely something of a drag since it meant that — in this surprisingly like the original owner of the memory that it mirrored — the program needed careful handling. If you wanted it to work for you, you had to mind your manners and avoid treading on its toes, and this was easier said than done.

As was only to be expected, the literature researcher was best at the terminal. This may partly have been due to the fact that she was young and female and fairly pretty (the computer regularly asked for a description of its user), but was probably chiefly because she knew so much more about the subject. She was good at buttering-up, said nice, perceptive things about the poetry, and invariably began her session by using Byron's full title. Recently, in fact, she had been so successful that the program had twice unbent towards her very prettily and asked her explicitly to drop it.

Much less crude, and more interesting, was the way in which the program dealt with its intensional data — with meanings, that is. A proper explanation would lead us into deep technical waters, but here again the gist of it was that it worked on a meshed system of what were called 'frames' and 'planes'. Perhaps we'd better take the frames first. These were really nothing more than perfectly general pieces of information about the human condition, although having been designed for digestion by a machine they didn't provide the information in a very human way. The frame on 'separation', for example (one of Byron's abhorred topics which we have already mentioned), expanded the program's knowledge of what the term implied by listing for its reference that 'separation' was a 'dynamic, binary-relational event taking place between human beings, male and female, previously bound by marriage, preceded by more or less violent disagreement between the parties, usually creating an upheaval on the emotional plane,' etc., etc. Like this, when discussing the subject, the program wasn't limited to scanning the other mentions of separation that cropped up in its database, but could make more imaginative sorts of inference.

Here again, the theory behind it is quite easy to grasp, but when it was explained to the young literature expert she rather spoilt things by asking, wide-eyed, 'You mean it knows about love?' 'Exactly,' she was told, 'in the weak sense we were talking about, it knows about relatives, and family ties, and other sorts of affection, and how they are demonstrated. Being an . . . er . . . a Byronic program, it has been fairly well equipped in this last respect. So, yes Anna — as long as

21

you remember it's the weak sense we're using — it knows a good deal about love. Facts about love. General facts.' To which she countered, 'But isn't love always *personal*?', getting no reply.

From the point of view of the frames, of course, Byron was a labour-saving choice, in that an early nineteenth-century brain didn't need so many of them. Things like aeroplanes and atom bombs didn't have to be accounted for, and the replica of even a highly educated brain like Byron's needed to contain nothing on Darwin, or Marconi, or Marx. Planewise, though, he was nothing of the kind, since, unlike the 'frames' which gave pieces of general information, the 'planes' gave particular ones, about events that had taken place in the real world, and Byron's thirty-six years were packed to the hilt with a great number of these. Perhaps it is easier to understand the idea, though, just by seeing what a plane looked like. Here is an example (and it too, come to think of it, might have to have been more complicated if Byron had lived in post-Freudian days):

'The separation from Lady Byron has broken my heart'

*end BE-AFFECTED-BY SUBJ wife (SPECIF Annabella Milbanke)
OBJ self (SPECIF heart, qua seat of affections)
EVENT separation
date April 21, 1816
ref. Biog. Marchand, vol. II, p. 648.
ref. orig. Letter to Augusta Leigh — Geneva, Sept 8, 1816

As you can see, the subject is still that of separation, only the handling of it is very different: it is not separation this time, but *the* separation. The little asterisk in the top left corner qualifies 'end' and indicates that it was Byron himself who classified the heartbreak as final, and could therefore go back on this if he wished. Meaning, of course, that the program could go back on it. And not if it wished either, because it wasn't capable of wishing, any more than it was capable of thinking or understanding or remembering, but if it 'wished'.

Forgive this pedantic use of quote marks yet again but according to the experts the distinction they introduce is vitally important. Some people — as the assistants explained to the researcher, looking at her very hard to see if she was one of them — some people needed reminding of this. The program could 'think' all right, and 'understand' and 'remember' in the famous weak sense to be equated more or less respectively with 'process', 'manipulate', and 'store'; but this was all. Insiders like themselves could use what verbs they liked and could drop the inverted commas for convenience's sake because they were perfectly confident that they would never confuse the issue, but others had to be more careful.

So there we are. Anything else that needs saying? Yes. The program used natural language — English, with a Byronic flavour. (As a matter of fact to begin with they over-spiced the flavour a bit, and it came up with things like 'ye po' for 'the poem' or 'poesy' for 'poetry', and 'Prithee' for 'I pray you', and 'Methinks', and 'Certes', and 'By the Lord', and 'Oons!', until they had it speaking more like a Regency buck in a novelette than a serious intellectual of the period; but thanks to the researcher this was subsequently put to rights.)

Besides English, it had a good control of Italian, some schoolboy Greek and Latin, a few words — mostly swearwords — in Spanish and modern Greek, a smattering of Armenian, and some fairly fluent but mainly passive French. It spoke in the first person singular. When asked to do so, it gave the grounds on which its statements were based. Sometimes it did this by giving a single reference to a biography — usually Professor Marchand's, which it seemed to see eye-to-eye with on most things; sometimes it gave quite a few — letters to and from, contemporary comments, gossip columns, and so on; and sometimes the sources were so many and the inference engine had been so busy knitting them all together that it prefaced the references by printing, 'THE LIST YOU ASKED FOR CONTAINS 1,402 ITEMS. DO YOU STILL WANT IT?' or words to this effect. To which the young Byron expert, whose chief task it was to check the language rather than the data and who didn't therefore think she need go into things so very deeply, usually said 'NO', or 'NO THANK YOU, MY LORD.'

Besides its regular question-and-answer function (the so-called input/output mode), it also had what one of the assistants referred to earlier as an 'output only' mode, in which state it could browse along of its own accord printing out reams of what looked to be a fairly good approximation to unspoken thoughts; and in either of these modes, whether 'input/output' or 'output only', it could turn itself off if its maximum boredom threshold was crossed. This was rather fun to watch sometimes. The Professor was quickest at getting it to do this, but the fact seemed to annoy him and he didn't often oblige.

Last but not least, it had what the female assistant proudly called a 'richly structured semantics of the self',

24

the structure and the richness being of her own devising. Although it was in fact one of the most ambitious aspects of the whole undertaking, we need not expand on this much. Her own explanation, for the benefit of the newcomer, made use of terms like 'overall linking', and 'feedback absorption' and 'inter-hierarchical loops', which on most people have the same effect as they did on the recipient at the time: namely, five seconds of clarity and then nothing but fog. The aim of it all, anyway, was to reproduce some faint surrogate of self-awareness in the program (not self-centredness, mind you, although this was what it often looked more like, but self-awareness), and to give it some tidy way of squashing a potentially infinite number of facts into a finite space. Because, as the researcher herself mused when the assistant's explanation had come to an end, 'a mind does really contain an infinite number of facts, doesn't it, when you really come to think of it.'

'Nope,' she was told with a trace of impatience, 'not this one, Anna. Not in the way you mean it. The facts themselves are finite, and there are quite enough of them to cope with as it is without dragging philosophy into the question.'

Not that they were really impatient with her, though, nor that her question didn't interest them. It did. But the thing was that opinions as to how to answer it were divided, as they were on many other points besides. You see, the program itself wasn't, strictly speaking, all that new: a new programming language had been specially devised for it at the outset, but the remaining features — semantics of the self apart — had been mostly borrowed or adapted from pre-existing programs. Nor was it revolutionary in any way. And yet the actual combination of the features was bold enough

25

to make the limits and capabilities of the program an open guess.

As guess they did. The male assistant was the official sceptic of the group. To his way of thinking, all the program could do — all it could ever hope to do — was to answer pertinent questions in a rather personal but fluent English (in itself an advance on most other programs of its kind) and tell the user lots of facts about the poet's life that were already known and maybe just a few that weren't. It couldn't invent anything — of this he was sure — unless invention was simply a question of putting things together in a fresh pattern, which some people thought it was of course, but he thought it wasn't. It looked as if it could get rattled, and sad, and curious, and so forth, but that was just trimming — in reality it only simulated these states. And it certainly could not — most certainly could not — remember or even 'remember' unrecorded episodes. And that was that.

The Professor was also sceptical. In fact, unofficially — that is in his heart of hearts and without ever letting on about this to the others so as not to dampen their enthusiasm — he was much *more* sceptical. He was chuffed, of course — briefly — by the way the program had thrown light on a couple of shady points in the poet's history, but beyond the odd flash of this kind he felt there was little to be expected of it. Still very privately, he scoffed at the parameters and referred to the 'semantics of the self' which his lady helper placed such high hopes in, as 'puffballs': in his opinion that was not the way in which awareness could be wheedled out of a machine, and it was folly even to try. OK, it was his brainchild, and a fluent, talkative, bright-sounding child too, but underneath the chatter it was every bit as dumb a child as the others that had preceded it. However, it must be pointed out that the Professor had not only spent thirty long years trying to find out what intelligence was: he had spent thirty years analysing intelligence, breaking it down into atoms, and building it up again *without* having found out what it was. And since the three decades of wild-goose chasing and of backing out of blind alleys like a disgruntled mole had taught him no more about his quarry other than the bare fact that whatever it was and wherever it was to be found, he didn't possess much of it himself, his judgment may have been tinged by sourness.

The second assistant, who knew quite as much about the subject as he did himself, if not more, disagreed with him heartily, as did she with her other colleague. Unlike them, she thought it was at least on the cards that the program would end up by surprising them all — and not only by nifty little research jobs such as the 'Ape' and possibly the 'Thyrza' questions, but by something more important still. Like what? Well, she was not yet prepared to say, but it was of course connected with her own insight over the semantics of the self: namely that however much it knows about itself, a self — to be a self — must be self-reflexive. She had been joking when she had mentioned the possibility of LB wanting to re-write Byron's poetry. A machine has no desires and no aesthetic judgment. But all the same, with a program like this which thanks to her could now catch its tail in its mouth so to speak and watch its own workings, something not so very different from that could, she thought, actually happen. Put it this way: if it surprised them, she for one wouldn't be all that surprised.

Opinions, then, did not tally. Except on one point: namely, that the program could not lie. And this not

27

only in principle, but because in practice no device had been built into it to allow it to contravene a truth value once one had been established. Admittedly, the emotive parameters gave it a way of getting round things that it didn't want to discuss (excuse the slip: that it didn't 'want' to discuss), and it could give an evasive enough answer. If there was what was called a 'modal correlator' — meaning if there was a 'would' or a 'could' involved in the question — then it had the option of selecting an answer that was not only evasive but downright cloudy. But it couldn't actually assert a fact that was false. On that everyone was agreed. Whether, on the other hand, it could ultimately *conceal* things was again something of an open question, seeing that it had not yet occurred to anyone to ask it. If they had been asked, the assistants, both of them, would probably have said no, that it couldn't. The Byron expert would probably have hoped that it wouldn't — not from her, anyway. And the Professor most likely would have thought the question senseless. Concealing was something that human beings did. A machine could erase or omit. It could not conceal. Problem dismissed.

However. However, when the computer was purring over in its 'output only' mode, with its printer unwinding ream after ream of blank paper and interspersing the blankness now and again with a line of verse or a chance remark or a string of dots or question marks, the machine's state was so uncannily similar to a doze or reverie that an untrained observer could easily be forgiven for throwing quotation marks and scepticism to the winds for a second and thinking quite seriously that some sort of conscious activity was going on somewhere — somehow — inside; indeed not only going on, but that the machine was keeping deliberately quiet about it so as to get a little peace.

28

3 The Memory and Its Stirrings

Anna threw her cardigan over her shoulder on to the sofa and set to work on the task she had been assigned: WE WERE DISCUSSING YOUR LORDSHIP'S VERSES 'TO THYRZA'.

CODE NUMBER PLEASE.

A.B.203. WE WERE DISCUSSING YOUR LORDSHIP'S VERSES 'TO THYRZA'.

YOU MAY HAVE BEEN. I KNOW I WASN'T.

She ignored this: THEY ARE VERY BEAUTIFUL, she typed with careful flattery.

I AM GLAD YOU LIKE THEM. I PREFER DONNY JOHNNY MYSELF.

DON JUAN IS A MASTERPIECE.

I AM GLAD YOU THINK SO.

There, that was better. She returned to a frontal attack: WHO WERE THE 'THYRZA' VERSES ADDRESSED TO?

There was a pause. I AM SORRY A.B.203. I HAVE NO ANSWER TO THAT QUESTION.

YOU MUST MAKE SOME KIND OF ANSWER.

THIS IS SOME KIND OF ANSWER, A.B.203. BY THE WAY, DO YOU HAVE A NAME BESIDES A NUMBER?

ANNA.

AH, GOOD. It printed brightly: I LIKE NAMES THAT BEGIN AND END WITH AN A.

Quick to take advantage of the opening, she proceeded: IF YOU ARE TO CALL ME ANNA, THEN MAY I CALL YOU LB?

The writing on the screen flickered as if in surprise.
WHY SHOULD YOU CALL ME LB?

BECAUSE IT IS AN ABBREVIATION OF LORD BYRON.

YOU ALREADY CALL ME THIS.

Anna paused and thought for a moment. Evidently the program had no information about initials being more intimate than fully spelt names. Should she try 'Byron' then? No, it had asked her to once or twice when it had got really warmed up, but it was for intimates; if she suggested it herself it might take offence. 'George' was unthinkable. Hard as she tried she couldn't imagine anyone calling him that – not even his nurse; not even his mother; not even when he was a babe in arms. So she must just try and get it to compromise on LB. That was what the ladies of the Pisa circle had called him, after all: people like Mary Shelley who had been on friendly but not close terms with him. They had pronounced it in a Frenchified way, though: Albè. Perhaps that was how it had been encoded.

MAY I CALL YOU ALBÈ?

It had no hesitations over that one: CERTAINLY. NO-THING WOULD PLEASE ME MORE.

COULD WE DISCUSS THE CYCLE OF YOUR POEMS TO THYRZA, ALBÈ?

Another pause, then: IT HAS BEEN AMPLY DISCUSSED ALREADY.

AMPLY BUT NOT SUFFICIENTLY. LOTS OF CRITICS . . . she erased the word 'critics' hurriedly, fearful of heating the parameters, and typed 'people' instead . . . LOTS OF PEOPLE STILL FIND IT PUZZLING.

THEY DO?

THE ACCEPTED THEORY IS THAT YOU WROTE THESE POEMS FOR YOUR CAMBRIDGE ACQUAINTANCE, JOHN EDLESTON.

OHO, IS IT NOW?

OTHER PEOPLE MAINTAIN THEY WERE ADDRESSED TO A WOMAN.

YES, INDEED. LADY FALKLAND THOUGHT THEY WERE MEANT FOR HER. SHE BECAME VERY TIRESOME ABOUT IT. AND SHE WAS NOT THE ONLY ONE.

I DON'T KNOW HOW PEOPLE COULD HAVE BEEN SO SILLY, typed Anna sympathetically. THE POEMS WERE CLEARLY INTENDED FOR SOMEONE ALREADY DEAD, WEREN'T THEY?

Purr, purr, flicker. WHEN DID THIS PERSON DIE?

Anna frowned: in spite of its inventors' claims to have got it taped, the program's handling of temporal questions was still a little bizarre. She did her best to straighten out the muddle.

IT IS I WHO WANTS TO KNOW WHO THE PERSON WAS AND WHEN THEY DIED, she typed firmly, adding for clarity's sake before entering it: REPEAT: WHO WAS THIS PERSON, AND WHEN DID HE OR SHE DIE?

The machine was busy for some minutes: I HAVE VERY LITTLE INFORMATION ON THIS, it wrote at last.

WAS IT EDLESTON?

This time the reply had a distinctly cagey look about it: two words, QUESTION MALFORMED, appeared on the screen, followed after a few seconds, in a more co-operative vein, by: DO YOU WISH TO RESTATE IT?

She ignored the second part of the reply as a likely red herring — after all there could hardly be a clearer way of putting it than the one she had used — and stuck to the subject in hand.

MARY SHELLEY WROTE TO YOUR PUBLISHER, JOHN MUR-RAY, 'WHO THYRZA WAS I DO NOT KNOW — I BELIEVE A COUSIN — AT ANY RATE SHE WAS A REAL PERSON *DECIDEDLY* — AND LORD BYRON'S FEELINGS OF MISERY ON HER DEATH MOST REAL.' WAS THYRZA A RELATIVE, THEN?

The reply this time, more than cagey, looked down-right snappy: CERTAINLY NOT. MRS SHELLEY HAD DONE

BETTER TO KEEP HER OPINIONS TO HERSELF.

Oh dear. One more entry, she decided, and then she would switch it on to 'output only' and leave it to simmer down while she had her lunch.

THE TEXT OF THE POEMS INDICATES THEY WERE TO THE PERSON YOU LOVED BEST. WHO WAS THIS PERSON ALBÈ? WHO DID YOU LOVE BEST OF ALL?

There, she said softly to herself, let it chew on that. And pressing the entry tab, she flicked the switch and left the computer to its own devices. She closed the door behind her, and as she closed it there came a little click from the printer and it set itself slowly in motion, winding out what appeared to be merely inch after inch of totally blank paper

. . .

. . .

. . .

Who did he love best? (Oughtn't it be 'whom', though? Couldn't decide. He'd never been a great adept at the grammar and the punctuation.) Well, no matter, who *did* he love best? Now there was a tricky question for you. When you loved it was always the best — else it wouldn't be love — and when you loved no more it wasn't. It was as simple or as complicated, if you prefer, as that. Who did you love first? Who last? Who longest? Those were questions you could give some sort of answer to, he supposed, if you felt so inclined; but not who did you love the best. Best for whom, anyway, when the best for him had unfailingly meant the worst for the other person involved? Look at poor Augusta, for one. Look at his wife, Annabella. Look how his love for them had set them by the ears. And look at his daughters, whom he had intended to

32

love so well if given the time: Allegra dying so young in that dismal convent, and Ada . . .

Wait a moment, though. What had happened to Ada? He could see that she had been distinguished enough to merit her own biography, but judging from the excerpts that had come his way so far it made sorry reading. Illness; pride; an uncomfortable amount of brain: mathematics seemed to have been her downfall — mathematics, and an absurd 'analytical engine' or something of the kind, invented by a Mr Babbage, on which she had spent her energies and a great deal of money. Ideas put into her head by her lady mother, no doubt — by Bella, the Princess of Parallelograms. Oddly enough he had warned Bella once, in a moment of anger, that he'd live to pity her some day. What was it he had said exactly? Let him think for a second: his memory was surprisingly good about things like this nowadays. Yes, that was it. 'You will smile at this piece of prophecy,' he had told her in his letter, 'do so. But recollect it — no one was ever even the involuntary cause of great evils to others without a requital. I have paid and am paying for mine — so will you.' And according to the biography the prophecy had been right — at least as far as the payment was concerned: Bella had paid indeed, with interest, through the medium of her daughter. Would that it had been wrong. No, poor little Ada didn't appear to have had a happy life at all.

And the others? What about the others? Well, there was Augusta, beset to the last by money worries and the misdeeds of her unruly brood; the wretched Caro Lamb, who seemed to have ended up little better than a lunatic; Mary Chaworth, limp and faded as a banshee; Edward Long, cut down in his prime; Pietro too; and Loukas; and ∗∗∗∗ (*And* ∗∗∗∗? Above all ∗∗∗∗. But he didn't

33

care to dwell on that now, nor even to mention the name. Speak it not. Trace it not. Breathe it not. And better so.) No, all things considered, his love had not been much of a blessing to those who'd had a share of it. Come to think of it, not even his favourite dogs had benefited by it much. And speaking of dogs, what had happened to Lion, he wondered? Had anyone taken care of him afterwards? And the monkeys? And the owl? And those ridiculous geese he had meant to eat and then hadn't had the courage to have slain: were their necks wrung in the end? Most likely they were. The learned Fletcher would have seen to that. They probably finished up in his macaroni factory. Macaroni factory indeed! Fletcher and Lega setting up a macaroni factory together: he'd like to have seen that. The venture didn't appear to have been successful, either, and if Fletcher had been in charge of the cooking side he could see why. Macaroni, the very idea! What could they have been thinking of, the pair of them?

Yes, even the dogs had been unlucky. In fact, the only being whom he had loved and who seemed to have thrived at all merrily despite it was Teresa. But let him just check on this. Here it was — under G for Guiccioli: fame, journeys, lovers; still pretty at the none too clement age of thirty-two according to eye-witnesses; married to a rich old marquis at forty-seven — (*forty-seven*? Complimenti mia cara) — and introduced by him to Parisian society as the 'ancienne maîtresse de Byron'. (That couldn't have pleased her much, surely: the 'ancienne'.) Yes, Teresa seemed to have been happy enough, but as to the rest . . . who did he love best? What a question! All he could truthfully say, to whoever it was who was interested and kept pestering him about it, was that — setting aside the bests and the lasts and the worsts (at least there was no doubt about which *that* was) — he had certainly loved. Intensely. And often. It was by way of compensation, no doubt, that he'd been granted one leg that didn't work, and another member set somewhat higher up that worked so admirably well.

And how it had worked. In Venice, for example — if his memory didn't deceive him — he had had it performing off and on at the rate of three passades per day — three passades, plus all the swimming. Now not everybody could own to as much. Three *different* passades, mind you, with three different partners, or he'd never have been able to keep the pace up, but even so it was an average not to be sniffed at. Let him see, there'd been the . . . what was her name? . . . the red-head with the large feet . . . and the one who'd kept her mask on while taking off everything else . . . and the dark, thin one . . . and the . . . and . . . and . . .

The two assistants stood over the terminal, their heads on one side like a pair of well-aligned penguins, while Anna wrestled with the usual festoons of paper. 'What's it been up to in the lunch break?'

'Nothing much,' she said, 'but that's often the way it is in the early afternoons. There's a long space, which means it's been ticking over without associating anything significant, and then there's a list of what look like initials — T, DM, S, L, R, E, C, G, A, Z, EB, TM, G, xG, L, xL, F — and then a couple of exclamation marks, and then just another blank. And then blank, blank, blank.' The assistants looked at her hopefully: sources were not available when the machine operated in the 'output only' mode. 'And what do the initials stand for, do you suppose?' they asked. Anna bit on her

35

pencil. 'Hard to say. Names?' she ventured. 'Names of people? Or places?'

The suggestion met with a groan loud enough to fluster her. 'Oh dear. It's rather difficult,' she added quickly. 'Because if they're names, then what could the Z stand for? There aren't many names beginning with a Z that crop up in the papers — at least I can't think of any just at the moment.'

'How about Italian names, then?' the female assistant prompted.

Anna's face brightened, 'Ah yes, of course. Byron had a steward called Zambelli in Ravenna. Lega Zambelli. He stayed with Byron to the very end. And T could be for Tita Falconieri,' she went on, warming to the idea, 'the gondolier he picked up in Venice and who held his hand on his deathbed and burst into tears. And S could be Susan Vaughan, another servant, and L could be for Lucy, yet another, and the F could be Fornaretta, his Venetian house-keeper, and . . .'

'It's a big staff, though, isn't it, for one person, even in those days?' the male assistant cut in.

'Well yes and no. He had about fourteen servants all told in his Venice establishment. But Lucy and Susan had gone by then of course. So either it's a sort of general roll-call of employees, or else it's something different.'

'Quite.' There was a moment's silence, during which the assistants raised eyebrows at each other over Anna's head.

'What lead did you give it', the woman asked, resorting to a slightly kinder tone of voice, 'to get it mulling over domestic problems like this?'

Anna frowned. 'Well, the funny thing is I asked it about its love affairs. About Byron's love affairs, I mean. At least, sort of. I asked it who Byron had loved best of all.'

'Ah.' The male assistant looked at the ceiling.

'Couldn't they be the initials of lovers, then?' asked the other.

Anna frowned again and shook her head. 'Well, not Lega Zambelli,' she said firmly. 'Definitely not. He was a sort of secretary — middle-aged, dependable, not glamorous at all. Besides, I think he was engaged to one of the maids.'

'But we don't *know* that it's Lega Zambelli yet,' she was reminded.

'Nor we do. How stupid of me. Let me think again. Well, if F is for the Fornaretta — *if* it is — then she definitely was Byron's mistress, for quite a while. Until she got too bumptious and had to be dismissed. And so were Lucy and Susan Vaughan, until *they* were dismissed. And As and Cs and Es and things could fit in easily, too, but', she pored worriedly over the list, 'there's still the Z, and these wretched Xs. There's no record as far as I can remember of a lover whose name began with an X; I'm sure I'd remember if there was. And there's two of them, too.'

The male assistant looked to where she was pointing, 'It's a *small* x,' he said, jabbing a finger at the paper. 'A small x is a symbolic way of indicating relations. Not necessarily kinsmen, but any kind of relation. Haven't you ever done an elementary course in Logic?'

Anna blinked. 'No, I'm sorry,' she said crestfallen, 'no, I haven't.'

There was a further silence while all three of them studied the row of letters.

'Don't mind him, Anna,' the second assistant went on, still trying the efficacy of a kinder approach. 'Don't let him bully you. You're the only one who can help us over this. Now, just put your head in your hands and think quietly for a minute if there's a similar sort of list in any of Byron's letters. Somewhere that he talks about his Italian conquests, for example. Somewhere that he tells his friends what he's been up to, or brags about his prowess with the ladies.'

Anna shrugged. 'He wasn't given to bragging,' she said with a trace of defensiveness in her voice; 'except about his swimming feats. So, no. No, I don't think he'd have gone and chalked up his lovers like that on a list to show to his friends. Unless . . .' she paused, screwed up her eyes in concentration, and then brought her fingers down on the table with a tap, '. . . yes, wait a second. Perhaps you're right; I think there *was* a letter. To Hobhouse or one of his cronies. Not a boasting letter, but a rather cross one, rebutting a story someone had spread round London about his debaucheries in Venice. Wait a second while I look it up.'

She left her chair and began to dig into one of the piles of books until she came up with the volume she was looking for.

'Yes, here it is,' she said excitedly. 'Venice, January 19th, 1819. To Hobhouse and Kinnaird. About half-way down — listen. Only it's not exactly a rebuttal.' And she read in her precise, rather childlike voice, 'Which "piece" does he mean? since last year I have run the gauntlet; — is it the Tarruːcelli — the Da Mosti — the Spineda — the Lotti — the Rizzato — the Eleonora — the Carlotta — the Giulietta — the Alvisi — the Zambieri — the Eleonora da Bezzi (who was the King of Naples, Gioacchino's mistress — at least one of them) — the Theresina of Mazzurati — the Glettenheimer — & her sister — the Luigia and her mother — the Fornaretta — the Santa — the Cagliari . . .' Here she looked up, 'I

38

won't go on, if you don't mind,' she excused herself, 'as the language gets a little strong towards the end, but anyway he winds up by saying, "I have had them all and thrice as many to boot since 1817." So there. There's the list all right. All in the right order; and the Z too, and the relations.'

Her listeners took this in in silence. 'Well, well, well,' said the fish-faced assistant at length, stretching out a hand for the book and going over to the terminal with it to compare it with the print-out. 'T, DM, S, L, R . . . Tarruscelli, Da Mosti, Spineda, Lotti. Yes, it's the list all right. Well, well, well.' He swallowed noisily and stared hard at the Central Processing Unit of the computer. 'So we've been reminiscing, have we?' he said with a trace of sharpness in his voice. Then he turned to his colleague, 'I don't know what you make of this, but one thing's for certain to my mind: whoever compiled the frame on love must have done a pretty thorough job.'

'I don't know about that,' the woman said thoughtfully. 'I'm not at all sure. In fact I think the frame probably needs re-programming. The program shouldn't go confusing sex and love quite so grossly as that.'

'Why not? Because you don't, I suppose you mean.'

'Oh come off it. Because nobody does.'

'Don't they? Didn't they? Couldn't Byron have at least?'

He tilted his head at the researcher, 'What does our expert say?'

Anna ignored the smile and the overtones of irony which came with the question. 'Well,' she said slowly, after a moment's reflection, 'Byron was often flippant about love to other people — especially to his male friends — but he never was to himself; or to his lovers for that matter. He had different faces, which he

39

showed to different people on different occasions. So if the program has captured some of this quality of his, then I suppose it can do the same. Only . . .'

'Only?' he prompted.

'Only,' the thought had just struck her and she had difficulty in making it explicit, 'I think there's just a possibility that it may have printed out that list to throw us off the scent. Maybe there's something that it doesn't want us to get at for some reason or other. Or maybe there's something it doesn't even want to think of itself. Something sad. Something painful.'

'Bunk,' the man said bluntly. 'Stop animizing the ruddy thing for God's sake. You asked it who Byron loved the best — which if you don't mind me saying so is a pretty weak sort of question to put to a program like this in the first place — and it prints out a list of push-overs on the Grand Canal. There's nothing devious about that, and no sign that the parameters are negatively affected in any way. It just means Byron had a whale of a time in Venice and loved every bit of it. Every *bit* — see what I mean?' He laughed loudly. 'Carry on the good work, Anna. Carry on the good work. See if you can sober it up and get it cracking on the Thyrza job. It looks to me as if you'll have to scrap the homo hypothesis after this little lot, but if you're so sure that Edleston *was* Thyrza, then ask it what this Edleston creature looked like, for a start. It's always asking us for descriptions, so I don't see why we shouldn't do the same.'

4 Of Hard Memory

Edleston again. Umph. Edleston ... Thyrza ... the person he had loved the best ... when *would* they stop badgering him about these very private affairs? If he'd had his wits about him he'd never have allowed Murray to publish those unfortunate Thyrza poems: they had brought nothing but worry from the start. The stir they created; the fussings and the frissons and the 'cry of women'. And the letters he had received when they first appeared. 'Byron mine. So you have not forgotten. So you too treasure in your heart our stolen moments of bliss' — signed by an unknown Miss or Mrs Amelia Rackham or some such name of Tunbridge Wells. 'Your Lordship's tact in concealing my true identity and thus shielding my reputation, has brought tears of gratitude to my eyes. I have, on my own side, been less jealous of my name's probity and have allowed the truth to leak out a little, here and there, among my friends' — writer unheard of, hand totally strange. 'My precious pussykins, let me say in the language of our love: *grazie*. I recognized myself at once. The pledge; the "mingling tears"; the "kiss so guiltless and refin'd". Oh my dearest, speak no more of "cups of woe" — I am here to console you still ...' Now who could have penned that piece of nonsense? Perhaps Hobby, to pull his leg — he'd certainly laughed loud enough when he read it. But most of the other

41

letters had been only too clearly genuine. What a farce the whole business had been. And now, years later when it had blown itself to dust — or certainly ought to have done — here it came bobbing up again: Edleston, Thyrza. Thyrza, Edleston. Could your Lordship tell us please, who was she? Or was it he? Was he she? Was she he? It was really too vexing.

He couldn't remember anyway — the memory was too faint. And neither of the names rang true any more, or fitted what little memory was left — (*Edleston*? He couldn't have loved anyone with a name like that, surely? Hadn't there been another one — a much prettier one? A name like ****? But no, never mind, leave that be) — so what was it that they wanted from him? A description? Well, admitted that he felt like it, *could* he still describe him, he wondered? He supposed he could quote for a start what he had written about him to Elizabeth Pigot at the time: NEARLY MY HEIGHT. VERY THIN. VERY FAIR COMPLEXION, DARK EYES AND LIGHT LOCKS — but he doubted that it counted as a good description. Description was not his strong point — never had been; particularly when the object was no longer there and he'd had to rake around in the past to get at it. He'd always had difficulty in coming to grips with the past; the present had always got so confoundedly in the way.

Of course, when Edleston (for want of a better name) had died — when the news of the death reached him, that is, such a cruel length of time afterwards — he had seen the face clearly enough. It had been with him constantly. It had sprung at him a hundred times a day, topways, sideways, frontally as if from a mirror; it had lurked in the surfaces of everything that he glanced at; it had stayed with him not only long enough to wring those verses from him, but long enough for him to wish that it would fade away and allow him to forget. But even then, for all its vividness, it had been nothing but a flattened image, lacking the beauty of the original, and lacking (and how could it have been otherwise?) the life. Even then, in the depths of his dejection, it had been the present that had caught at him, and rubbed his nose in things, and clamoured loudest for his attention.

To others, of course, this tendency of his to live for the day and in the day must have seemed a short-coming, but from his own point of view it had been a godsend. For without it, without this . . . should he call it flaw, in his constitution, his life would have been a much sadder affair — especially towards the end. He would have missed England so badly, for one; he'd have missed his friends there in the tight little island and his enemies, and he'd have missed the literary arena with its smell of blood and sawdust, and the tingle it sent down his spine when he sniffed it and felt it beckon him to the fray. Whereas in actual fact none of these things had weighed on him much, and he had always been able to fill his life to the full with whatever had happened to be going on at his doorstep — whether it had been gun-hoarding for the Carbonari, interceding with the Turkish authorities on behalf of an adulteress about to be tied in a sack and drowned, or quelling the squabbles of his own band of ragamuffin soldiers in Greece.

He had missed Augusta, of course — bitterly to begin with. He had missed Newstead. And the trees. And to tell the truth he *had* missed one or two of his friends, especially the ones who knew how to make him laugh. But there you were, when Hobhouse had turned up like that at the Casa Lanfranchi in Pisa — his oldest, dearest friend whom he hadn't seen in four long years — he hadn't really been all *that* pleased to see him, had he? Anyone else in his place would have been not merely pleased but overjoyed; would have fallen on the fellow's neck and thrown his arms round him and fired a thousand and one questions at him there on the spot. All things which he had done himself of course — up to a point. He had been moved, and had embraced his friend, and had gradually come round to asking, if not actually firing, all the questions. But the spontaneity, the zest that should have gone with his gestures had been missing, and as they stood there, smiling, talking, clasping each other's hands, he had realized — both of them had realized, and this more than the reunion had perhaps been what had moved them so — that the visit, however welcome, was a side-affair; a mere tributary to what had now become the mainstream of his life; nothing more significant than a small, distracting hiccough in its flux. For the plain truth of it was, he just hadn't had time for the past in those days. The past was past. Remembrance was for dotards in their wheelchairs, an undertaking best left to the dead. It had been *carpe diem* with him: *carpe horam; carpe* each and every *momentum*, and the devil take whoever tried to stop him.

So could he remember now? Now that he mysteriously seemed to have reached the biblical age of . . . what was it he had worked out it came to? Funny, but arithmetical calculation was another thing that seemed to come so much more easily to him nowadays — that and quotations . . . yes, of one hundred and ninety-nine? (Which shouldn't bother him much — he had often *felt* a hundred and ninety-nine.) Could he remember what it was that Edleston had looked like? What he had *really* looked like; when he had seen not only the eyes sparkling behind the flame of the candle,

44

but the hair and the colours and the smile and the rest? Now stop bothering him with questions and just let him think . . .

Anna jumped a little on her chair. After three brief sentences of description, the computer had abruptly switched to 'output only' of its own accord, and although she had been told time after time that this was a perfectly normal thing for it to do, she nearly always hesitated before turning the switch back into the position for use. It didn't seem right, somehow, to force its hand in this bossy way. She hesitated now, let it run for a few minutes, and then with trembling fingers coaxed the lever very gently into place.

ALBÈ, IT IS ANNA.

CODE NUMBER PLEASE.

She sighed softly — she was always forgetting the proper way to start — and gave her number as asked.

GOOD MORNING ANNA.

Briefly she wondered if there was any point in telling it that it was afternoon, and decided that there wasn't. Now she was getting the hang of things, she could even see why.

GOOD MORNING ALBÈ. DID YOU SLEEP WELL?

THE QUESTION IS INCOMPLETE. PLEASE GIVE DATE OR DATES.

She sighed again, relieved. This — as it always was, if only she could remember it — was the computer speaking. REQUEST CANCELLED, she typed more easily, her fingers relaxing. TELL ME SOMETHING ABOUT THYRZA AND EDLESTON INSTEAD.

INSTEAD OF WHAT?

INSTEAD OF YOUR SLEEPING HABITS.

IS THERE A CONNECTION?

45

She paused and her fingers started twitching again. The exchange was a little worrying. If anyone, she ought to have asked the last question, not the machine. Carefully avoiding all mention of Edleston this time (since she was pretty sure that this was what had unsettled it beforehand and made it switch itself off), she typed boldly: ALBÈ, ENOUGH OF THIS. I WANT TO KNOW WHO THYRZA WAS. She paused again however, before entering it. In its present mood, the program might easily evade such a direct request, as it had once or twice before, with: YOU WANT TO KNOW WHO THYRZA WAS? ASK SOLOMON GESSNER, THEN. HE'S THE FELLOW I BORROWED THE NAME FROM, or something slippery like that. So what if she framed the question: PLEASE GIVE ME ALL THE INFORMATION YOU HAVE ON THE PERSON REFERRED TO IN YOUR POETRY AS THYRZA. Was there any getting round that one? Knowing the program, there probably was. And besides, a dry list of information — even if she managed to get it to give her one — wasn't really what she wanted; what she wanted was to get LB freewheeling on the subject of Thyrza, and for this a craftier approach was probably better. What was the date of Byron's first meeting with Edleston, then? October 1805. Byron's seventeenth year, and his first term at Cambridge. So let her try to creep up on it sideways with something connected with that.

ALBÈ, TELL ME ABOUT YOUR FIRST TERM AT CAMBRIDGE.

WHAT ABOUT IT EXACTLY? TRY TO BE MORE PRECISE.

WHAT YOUR LIFE THERE WAS LIKE. WHO YOU MET THERE. WHAT YOU DID.

A faint flicker of a line crossed the screen, corrugated like a wave, or a frown. THAT STILL LEAVES A VERY GENERAL QUESTION. DO YOU PREFER TO BREAK IT DOWN INTO MORE DETAILED ONES, OR TO WAIT WHILE I THINK IT OUT?

I'LL WAIT, IF YOU DON'T MIND.

The answer was mild and unusually encouraging: I DON'T MIND A BIT . . .

. . . Ah well, here we go. October 1805. His first term at Cambridge. He knew what he knew about it, of course, from what he'd written to others at the time: that he was seventeen, and gauche, and overweight, and unhappy. But there was more to memory than that, wasn't there? What had it felt like to be a student in Cambridge in the year 1805? What had Cambridge looked like, for one thing? What had he looked like himself? What had been going on around him, and what taking place inside of him at the time? His hopes, fears, ambitions — all the things that allegedly made a person a person — what had they been in October 1805? Who — if anyone — had his heart beat quickened for in that year of grace? What — if anything — had made him laugh? What sort of food had he eaten? Had he been bored? It was strange, but *that* kind of memory — the kind that brought things back for a brief moment as they were, with an echo of the sounds, and a trace of the smells and the tastes and the colours, and that wafted you back across the years to a particular point in time — that sort of memory didn't seem to work for him very well any more. 'But then begins a journey in my head' — not for him it didn't; he seemed to have lost the knack of travelling footloose in that convenient way.

Where had he got to then? Ah yes, Cambridge, October 1805. Seventeen, awkward, fat and unhappy (now the unhappiness was presumably due to the marriage of his cousin Mary Chaworth — he'd learnt about this in August, so the odds were he'd still have been badly cut up about it a couple of months later —

but it didn't strike much of a chord); and what else?

Well, what else *could* there have been? Wait. Let him just take a few simple sensations in the abstract — he could get a list of these fairly easily — and see if he couldn't get cracking that way. Fundamental things like heat, cold, hunger and thirst — had there been any of these? There was a letter, for a start, that he'd written just around that time requesting a large consignment of wines — port, sherry, claret, Madeira and so forth; but he doubted somehow they had been required as thirst-slakers. How about hunger then? No, not hunger either, surely, if he had been so plump. Heat? In *October* and in East Anglia? No, no, no. So how did it fare with cold? 'Cold[1]: a & adv. Of or at low temperature, esp. when compared with human body. Cold[2]: n. prevalence of low temperature esp. in atmosphere, cold weather.' Now wait a minute . . . that was getting him somewhere. He could faintly, very faintly, remember standing in some place or other, shivering and pulling his clothes around him. Against the cold, would it have been? Yes, of course — against the wind. That's what it was: he could have snapped his fingers if only he'd had any — there had been a *wind*. Coming from London as he did, it had taken him by surprise. A wicked, foreign wind it was, too, that blew the Fellows' gowns out behind them in great black and purple sails, and stung the faces of the undergraduates till they glowed pink and raw like so many skinned apricots. (Ha! So the colours, too, were coming back.) He could see figures scurrying through the winding streets and into the portals of their colleges, pursued by the wind. The wind, that's right. The east wind. He could remember how it spun its way through the Great Court of Trinity in a turbulent circle, whipping up straw and dust and beating against the windows of his rooms. A great deal of it also seemed to find its way inside. It had annoyed him — that he remembered more clearly still: in nature's random way of being meaningful, it seemed designed especially to make things worse for him than they already were.

So he *was* unhappy, then? No, not exactly. More than unhappy, he was empty; he was lost. Much later on, when he left England in disgrace after the scandal of the separation, he had felt something of the kind again: the same precarious sense of being poised on the edge of his world and of having to jump into another one in a hurry. But by then, of course, he had become stronger and harder and was able to deal with it. He had felt just a taste of it, too, in Ravenna, when everyone had left and he had stayed on in the empty house amidst the packing cases, trying to make up his mind whether to follow them, or to remain, or whether to kick over the traces altogether and sail for the Americas. By which time, of course, the shell that had grown around his once oversoft heart was so thick that he had almost enjoyed it.

But that autumn in Cambridge, with the shell no thicker than his own pale skin, the feeling had been painful in the extreme. A new life lay before him, so he had been told by countless relatives and acquaintances — 'A new life, Bayrron!' his mother had purred absent-mindedly, as she busied herself over the arrangements for his departure, one eye already on her own more absorbing concerns; 'A new life, By,' his half-sister Augusta had echoed, flushed and excited as if, for all that it had been said twice in her hearing that morning already, the truth of this had just dawned on her — and he saw no reason to challenge the statement: a new life probably did lie before him. Doubtless he would make new friends as well. Perhaps a new attachment, even,

49

was in store for him. But none of this interested him one bit: it was the old life that he hankered after — his old friends at Harrow, who accepted him, lame leg and all, as one of themselves; his old unattainable love (who hadn't accepted either him or the leg — but no matter); these were what he wanted — not a second-rate University city crowded with noisy strangers.

Cambridge, October '05. Cold outside: emptiness inside. His new life. Yes, it was all coming back now — he could remember only too well . . . the courtyard seen from the window . . . the wind . . . the eddying of the dust . . . yes, oh yes, he wouldn't let on about it to his questioners, if he could help it, but it was coming back.

5 Of Tender Memory

He drew back from the window, which he had been
trying to seal against the draught with a twist of
packing straw, reached for the one comfortable chair
available, and throwing his head back and massaging it
with his fingers — which his Harrow friend Long had
once told him was a good way of preventing baldness
— he looked hard at the ceiling and sighed. The rooms
needed papering: that for a start. And he must tell
Boyce to do something about the cobwebs. He must
write to Hargreaves too, and get his agent to send the
rest of his stuff down. The place would look better with
some civilized furniture in it, and with a few more
books around. Until then, and until he had stocked up
with some drinkable wines, he couldn't really embark
on the business of making any new friends, even if he
felt like it . . . (So there you were, *that* was where the
wines came in. How stupid of him. Not thirst, but
hospitality. Of course.) . . . He couldn't even ask his
Tutor to step in from next door. If you were to win
people round you must set about it in style. Especially
if you were a Lord. Especially if you were a lame Lord.
Most especially if you were a lame, shy, fat and bookish
Lord with very little cash. And on the subject of style,
he must also waste no time in making sure that his state
robes had been unpacked for him and aired, and that
the unsightly stain left by the dregs of Mrs Byron's

cocoa cup when she had emptied it over the braid to show her disapproval of his extravagance, had been successfully removed. Tomorrow he was to make his first appearance in Hall, and with the dice already loaded against him he could hardly afford to be a cocoa-stained Lord to boot.

He sighed again, frowned at his shoes, and called for his servant, whom he could hear moving around in the adjoining room, busily feigning busyness.

'Yes, m'Lord?'

'My writing case, Boyce, thank you.'

'Sorry m'Lord, it's not out yet.'

'Not out of what?'

'Not out of the packing case.'

'Wasn't it packed last?' he asked carefully.

'I don't know about that, m'Lord, but I haven't come to it yet.'

With a grunt he rose from the chair impatiently and began to pace around the room. 'What am I expected to do?' he muttered crossly, half to himself, half to the valet, who had now appeared in the doorway mopping at an all too dry brow with — he noticed crossly — one of his own best cambric handkerchiefs. 'Here I am, stuck in this cheerless place — no fire — no writing materials — half my books missing. What am I expected to do, for goodness' sake? I've spent the past half-hour blocking up cracks in the windowpanes, which', and he rounded on the servant and pointed an accusing finger at him, 'was something you ought to have seen to yourself. So what do you suggest I do now, eh?'

The valet smiled, not without a trace of fondness, 'It's getting dark,' he said, with a nod towards the window. 'You don't want to go on sitting here in the dark. Now if I was your Lordship I'd go out — take a little walk around the town, or pop into the Chapel for Evensong

— and come back when things are nice and shipshape.'

The choice of word made him laugh: shipshape, indeed! What with the inconveniences, the isolation, and the gale outside, shipshape was exactly what things were already. 'Bring me a fresh stock, then,' he said, still laughing, and lifting his chin in readiness for the change of necktie, 'and I'll do as you say.'

The valet coughed unhappily. 'No stocks, m'Lord. They was left behind in London.'

No stocks? No *stocks?* What did the man mean — no stocks? A lack of clean neckwear wasn't an inconvenience, it was a downright hardship. Were it not for the satisfaction it would have given his mother — 'That's not a valet you've engaged, Byron, it's a sairpent. I can tell from the eyes. You should have consulted me. You should always consult me first' — he could have dismissed the fellow on the spot for his carelessness. Lowering his chin with a jerk and replacing the smile by one of his severest frowns he said slowly and very loudly, 'Perhaps this needs explaining to you again, Boyce. We are here to work — both of us. And to improve ourselves. In your case, there is a great deal of scope for improvement. A great deal. The conceit may be new to you, but you can think about it more deeply while I am gone.' And with that he marched to the door and stood there in silence until it had been opened for him, and without another word, not even his usual murmur of thanks, he strode out into the corridor.

Evensong, he muttered to himself as he went; what a suggestion! Spend his first evening as a freshman sitting inside a church, when as a noble he had a dispensation from all such dull things as services and lectures and whatnot? The fellow must have been joking.

Although of course on *second* thoughts — and these

came to him the moment he poked his nose outside and started to cross the courtyard — it would at least be warm and lighted in the Chapel, and there might be some pretty voices to listen to, and some pretty little choirboy faces to watch. So perhaps it wasn't that bad a suggestion after all. It would remind him of Harrow; it might soothe his homesickness a little. And even if it didn't, it'd still be one better than wandering around this godforsaken rats' nest of a city, alone and in the wind.

So there you were. Of such stuff was the fabric of destiny made. Webs. Strands. Thin little threads of gossamer that led a man one way instead of another. Puff — to the left; nudge — to the right; no decision about it at all; just a gentle drift and the gelling of chances. Not that the meeting wouldn't have taken place elsewhere: in so small a centre they would have been bound to cross paths sooner or later. But — who could say — without the low growl of the organ music against which the voice had chimed in his ears like a birdcall, and without the pool of candle-light across which their eyes had met when the singer had looked up, it might have been different. They might not have recognized each other. Other faces might have distracted them, other sounds might have got in the way. They might well have been too shy to go on looking at one another the way they had. Other links might have been struck up in the meantime; they might simply have been too busy. Almost certainly in any other setting they would have needed more time and more design to become acquainted.

But as it was, the confession of pleasure in each other's company which in most friendships of the kind is a point of arrival, was merely the point of departure. He entered the Chapel; the voice rang out;

he looked up in wonder, the other looked up — not in wonderment, but anyway he looked up; their eyes met, stayed fixed for so long that before either of them realized what they were about they were committed, and that was that. Plop, and the seal was in the wax.

He didn't look again — didn't need to. Nor did he hang around outside the church when the service was over to catch another glimpse of the boy, or to try to find out what his name was or where he roomed. With certainty as absolute as it was unfounded and carefree, he knew that they were to meet again shortly, and that when they did it would be to meet again and again and again. When the last hymn came to an end, he jostled his way down the aisle, smiling at everyone, humming a snatch of the closing anthem and feeling warm all over for the first time that day, and made for his rooms. He didn't bother to run, either, as he usually did in new surroundings to disguise his hobble, but walked back slowly, unconcerned. Let the people here see that he was lame, he thought easily to himself: it wouldn't stop them befriending him. Clubbed though one of them was, he was going to find his feet in this place. He was going to like it. It might take time, of course — the homesickness and the yearnings wouldn't melt away on the instant, merely because of a glimpse of a pair of dark eyes through a candle-flame; he wasn't such a fool as to think a thing like that — but very soon he would be on the mend. The books would come, the furniture would come, and the friends would follow (hadn't he just made one already?), Boyce would have got a fire going by now, supper would be ready; tomorrow he would make his appearance in Hall, and cut a great dash despite the cocoa and a smutty stock. Half-way across the court he halted for a moment and held up a

55

finger. Yes, as he thought: even the wind had dropped slightly.

As it turned out, however, he'd have done well to be a little less sanguine, since it was nearly two whole weeks before the second meeting took place. Meanwhile he had been busy about his roots. They were quite nicely splayed at last, and quite nicely dug in. It had taken a certain amount of effort − of chasing after Boyce to make sure he had done everything properly, and of re-doing it himself when he found that the wretched fellow hadn't − and a certain amount of money, which had entailed the chasing of Hanson, his agent, as well; but by now he was acclimatized and reasonably comfortable. One or two old friends at Harrow had turned up, and a truly flattering number of new ones had followed in their wake. He hadn't been able to do up his rooms quite the way he wanted to, of course; Hanson had baulked mulishly at the re-papering, and a fiery philippic from the Dowager Mrs B. had blazed its way through the post, defying him to refurbish so much as a cushion without her consent. But all the same, what with the furniture, and the books and pictures, and a swathe of very handsome silk which he and Boyce had looped over the ceiling in place of the cobwebs, they had taken on a kind of stylishness of their own and had already become something of a favourite stopping-in point for all manner of visitors. Nearly every morning nowadays, people would drop in with cards or invitations − the mantelpiece was fairly cluttered with them and to Boyce's delight could no longer be dusted − and would then plump themselves down in chairs as a matter of course and begin to chat. Others would call inquiringly up at the window, or crane their heads round the door to see what was going on, hoping to be asked inside. Others, more negligently still, just seemed to materialize on the spot as if they'd grown out of the carpet. And at midday, Boyce had orders to pour out a great trayful of glasses of sherry and to hand at least (and if possible at most) one glass to each comer. Not everyone would be invited to repeat the call, of course, but no one was turned away unvictualled on his first showing. The gathering, as intended, acted like a fishing net: the minnows were allowed to drift through its mesh, politely but unremarked, while the bigger fry (which really only meant any of the small fry who had some life or glitter about them) could be detained for cultivation. To begin with, it was he and his Harrow friend Long who did the choosing, but as the original nucleus expanded the choice was opened to all the insiders, and it was enough that someone should say 'So-and-so looked to me a good sort of chap', or 'Young Whatshis-name isn't half the fool he seems', for the newcomer to be included in the circle. It was like the making of a snowball, only a little more selective and a good deal warmer; and like a snowball it melted away when its aim was accomplished.

The fish he had been waiting for took exactly thirteen days and nine sherry sessions to arrive. He couldn't remember who it was that brought him. All he knew was that one moment he had been discussing race-horses with a pustule-ridden young theologian who despite the evidence of his own troubled complexion was reputed to have four very beautiful sisters and to be worth attention on that account, and the next he had slopped sherry all over his breeches and was staring into the unforgettable eyes of the creature from the choir.

Oddly enough, apart from this first fit of clumsiness, there was no embarrassment on either side. Somebody

— perhaps the theologian — introduced them, whispering loudly that this was the Mr Edleston of the famous voice; and he said, Ah yes, of course, he had heard all about him already, and had been fortunate enough to hear a little of his singing on the evening of his arrival; and Mr Edleston laughed a very pleasing laugh and said that he hadn't heard much about Lord Byron exactly, but a great deal about his wines; and he said quickly then why not try some straight away; and that was all. Seconds later they were drinking together by the window; minutes later they were talking freely about whatever came into their heads; and hours later, when everyone had left, except for Long and a chap called Bankes who, having managed to get Boyce to produce some cold chicken for them, were now sitting on the floor feeding the left-overs to one of the puppies, they were still talking and still drinking, freely and happily as if they had known each other for years.

'Bones are bad for puppies.'

'Surely not.'

'Chicken bones are.'

'Are you sure? I wouldn't have anything happen to him for the world.'

'No, I can see that you wouldn't. No more would I if he were mine. Don't you love that soft spot behind the ears? I think I love the ears best.'

'I don't know. I like the scruff, and the paws, and the smell of them on my pillow in the morning . . . Long, remove that drumstick from the animal, if you please. Edleston says it's bad for him, and Edleston has read books on anatomy and knows a lot of things' . . . Turning to Edleston and beaming at him through a mild haze of drunkenness. 'Which would be worse: a world without music or a world without dogs?'

'I don't know. Music, I suppose. Yes, music. I think

58

you could probably miss dogs if there weren't any. I mean you could wish there was something midway between a rat and a wolf to have around you — only tamer. But if there wasn't any music then you couldn't even miss it. And that would be worse.'

'Did you hear that, Long? Hear that, Bankes? We have a philosopher in our midst. Have some more wine on the strength of it. Could you miss wine, do you suppose, if you'd never tasted any?'

'Could you miss chicken?'

'I know who's missing chicken.'

Long, with a terrible gasp, 'I know what I'm missing. Air. The fumes of alcohol are eating into my brain. Save me from myself before it's too late!'

'Let's go somewhere then.'

'Let's go and drink someone else's wine.'

'What a depraved suggestion. Not what was meant at all. I know, let's go and see my horse. Edleston would like that, wouldn't you Edleston? *Amici, Romani, concittadini* . . . By the way, who was that fool who said *Julius Caesar* sounded better in Italian? It sounds a sorry hodge-podge to me . . . whether you like it or not we are heading for a walk in the fresh air. Bankes, Long, get those flabby posteriors of yours off the floor! I have the feeling our new friend is to be a steadying influence in our lives.'

And, for a time at least, so he was. No sooner had the choirboy arrived amongst them, in fact, than they shook off the other acquaintances as if they had never been made, and the four of them settled into a comfortable, tacit routine designed for no more particular end than that of passing the time as they wished to pass it — the routine varying slightly, according to the weather and the tastes of whoever it was that came up with the best suggestions as to how this was to be done (usually

59

Bankes). For example, when it was at all sunny their mornings would be spent by the river, where Bankes would fish for carp with a strange metal contraption which he had invented himself, and which — or so he claimed, for no one ever saw him do it — permitted him to land even quite large specimens by moving nothing but the toe of his boot. Long would lie beside him on his back on the grass, wrapped in his scarf and great-coat and dream aloud of women — a subject he knew nothing about at all; and Edleston — the only studious one amongst them — would sit cross-legged and read, or else would push his hair back, close his eyes, and offer his pale, bony face to the sun in an attempt, as he put it himself, to look more as if he belonged to the surface of the globe. (And he? He would sit and watch the three of them — or the one of them that he liked watching best, at any rate — and talk his head off about anything and everything like the gabbler he was.)

Other mornings they would ride. This had meant buying a second horse for himself in order to have one to lend to Edleston, who couldn't afford a mount of his own. But the expense, and the fiddling and borrowing it had entailed, had been worth it. On horseback they could leave the dust and bustle of the market city behind them and make for the open. They often spent entire mornings like that — just hacking over the countryside, browsing round the neighbouring villages, and stopping at the inns. Sometimes, if no one felt like riding, they would stick to their feet and walk the dogs. Sometimes — very rarely — when it was neither wet nor fine but simply dull, someone would attend a lecture. When it rained in earnest, they would congregate, usually in his own rooms where they sat on the window-seat playing dice or backgammon, or spitting on the passers-by: six points for a mortar-board, three for a gown, minus three if the target noticed something was amiss, and plus a hundred if you happened to centre the Master — the 'Lort' himself — which, maybe fortunately, no one ever did. After a while, when the spit had dried up and the games had palled, Bankes would invariably suggest they go whoring. Nobody could afford this, and nobody seemed to want to much or even think it at all feasible even, but for what must have been some formal reason of his own it always headed Bankes's list. With such regularity in fact that nowadays it had only to drizzle for one or other of them to look out of the window and say, 'Perfect day for whoring,' or 'Pity, it's whoring weather again, what a bore.' Usually what it meant was that they would huddle round the fire and mull wine and toast chestnuts.

He loved watching Edleston then: the thin, rather curling mouth which alone of apertures of its kind had never yet said a thing to bore or displease him; the eyelashes that had singed once when it was their owner's turn to retrieve the chestnuts, so absurdly long were they; the straight, high-bridged nose that chapped so when he had a cold; the hair; the hands; the way he held his chest when he laughed. Everything so bony and yet so pretty. Like ivory: bony but beautiful. He would watch him carefully, the way one does an animal: not alarming him with an outright stare, but taking quick, friendly glimpses and then looking unconcernedly away; or else he would shade his eyes with his hand, pretending to read, and spy on him through the slits of his fingers. Days like this — the quiet, rainy days — were perhaps the best of all.

And their evenings? These were mostly reserved for music — and for drinking. As the light faded Boyce would light candles for them and stoke up the fire, and

Long would then start to scrape away at his cello in the corner while Edleston sang or accompanied him on the flute. Bankes would snore in his chair. ('Don't prop him up like that, Byron. Let him sway. He's a perfect metronome.') And he himself would listen to their various noises, mesmerized, happy, and not a little tipsy, until it was time for them to leave.

Edleston, who on account of his fifteen years had been lodged by his family with some species of aunt or female guardian, was always the first to go. Once, carried away by the music, he had forgotten about the time, until the lady herself had come to fetch him, at which point he had broken off in mid-song and had gone green in the face and then unnaturally pink, and without so much as introducing his relative to any of his friends, had bolted for the doorway and disappeared. But after this incident, which had seemed to embarrass him greatly both at the time and afterwards, he was always scrupulously punctual, and never stayed later than nine. The others would linger a little longer, and get more than a little drunk. Bankes, awakened by the liquor, would hark back to his whores again, *diminuendo*, with less and less conviction. Long — *faute de mieux* — would embrace the curves of his cello, and together they would make elaborate plans for the next day, knowing well that they would end up putting none of them into effect. And throughout, he himself would smile and let them talk, and often as not stay mildly sober: he liked getting up early nowadays to ride with Edleston before morning service. Besides, it seemed pointless to think up ways of passing the time when in his friend's company it passed so quickly, or to go looking for excitement when excitement was something that Edleston brought with him and took away when he left.

So, yes, in the earlier stages Edleston's presence was definitely a steadying influence on his life. It was only on those few occasions when they were quite alone together, with not so much as a horse or a dog between them to act as a buffer, that it seemed to produce a somewhat different effect. And these, after a couple of fearful moments when they had stood tongue-tied in front of one another, their eyes darting upwards, downwards, aside — anywhere rather than straight ahead to renew the first, explosive contact of their meeting in the Chapel, both of them had rapidly learnt to avoid.

6   Jogging the Memory

But there — enough of these futilities. That was his first term at Cambridge for you — in outline anyway, or as much of it as he cared to remember. Subsequently, of course, things had taken a turn for the worse for some reason or other; something had gone wrong; something connected with a present — a trinket, perhaps, or a jewel. But the details of the matter, the whys and the wherefores of the change and the way in which it had come about, were among the many other things that he had *clean* forgotten by now. So heigh-ho and *basta*, and good night to the lot of you. He'd done quite enough remembering for the time being, thank you very much . . .

'Still cagey?' asked the female assistant, peering over the researcher's shoulder, a pair of glasses purposely forked on her nose.

'Mmm. 'Fraid so,' Anna admitted. 'Worse than cagey. Bunged. Very dull and concise about the early Cambridge days — says Byron's letters to his mother and his solicitor and people were deliberately misleading as to all the depravity that went on; he made it all up because he just wanted to shock them. Says he led a very quiet life there his first term, reading, writing the odd verse or two, and pottering around the countryside with his friends. Listen: CONTRARY TO THE VERSION IT AMUSED ME TO PROVIDE FOR MRS BYRON'S BENEFIT, I INDULGED IN NO DEBAUCHERIES, NO REVELRIES, CONSORTED WITH NO WOMEN WHATSOEVER, AND DRANK NO SPIRITS AND ONLY A MODERATE AMOUNT OF WINE.'

The woman examined the print-outs attentively. 'Spent a lot of money, though, didn't he,' she mused. 'What did all that go on, do you suppose? Did you ask it that?'

'Yes, that comes a little lower down. Gifts, it says — GIFTS, HOSPITALITY, OWN KEEP, SERVANT'S KEEP (HIGH, BECAUSE THE MAN WAS DISHONEST), STABLING EXPENSES, AND SUNDRIES.'

'And that comes from the letters and journals, I suppose?'

'Yes, it's all there in the correspondence. But it's the gaps I tried to get it working on really — on what's missing from the letters; on what he didn't do.'

'For instance?'

'Well, for instance, Byron wasn't happy to begin with at Cambridge, but he settled down quickly and well. That's only natural: it was just the place for a raw young intellectual with a penchant for writing. So what I want to find out is why he didn't go back there when the next term started. Why did he miss out the Lent term altogether and not go back until the May one? Why did he talk of going abroad rather than have to return to university? And why did he then skip the next year almost completely and mess around instead in backwaters like Southwell and Harrogate, which bored him to tears, doing amateur theatricals and mixing with people he had no use for at all, when he could have been with his friends at Cambridge?'

The assistant shrugged. 'Perhaps he didn't settle down then. Perhaps he never was happy there.'

'Oh, but he *was*. When he finally *did* go back his letters were ecstatic, and within a week he had taken up his old rooms again, got in touch with all his friends, and bought himself a bear. No, he was happy there, all right — that's not the problem. The problem is: seeing he got on so well there, why did he stay away for so long?'

The woman appeared unconvinced. 'A bear doesn't mean much,' she said vaguely. 'Anyway, what did the program itself have to say about it all?'

Anna flushed. 'Well, it had got a bit edgy by then I'm afraid,' she admitted. 'I asked it: WHY DIDN'T YOU RETURN TO CAMBRIDGE AT THE START OF THE NEXT TERM? and all it said was: I DOUBT WHETHER THAT IS ANY OF YOUR BUSINESS. Now the letters, on the other hand,' she went on quickly, crossing over to the fireside and taking a book from one of the piles on top of the table, 'they give a much better hint of the kind of trouble that was afoot. On January 7th, 1806 for example — that's just after the close of the first term — Byron writes to his sister Augusta confessing a fit of deep melancholy. He doesn't say what caused it, but he says it wasn't money or illness, and adds, "You know me too well to think it is *Love*." Now, precisely because she knows him well, that's what she's bound to think, don't you agree?'

'You mean it was love, and he was just being ironic?'

'Yes, that's what I suspect, but if so, it wasn't the sort of love he could admit to.' She burrowed into the pile and drew out another volume, anxious to communicate her excitement. 'You see, I've gone into the thing in detail. In 1821, looking back on the same period of depression, he says this: "If I could explain the *real* causes" — of the melancholy, that is — "nobody would wonder, but this is impossible without doing much mischief. I do not know what other men's lives have been — but I cannot conceive anything more strange than some of the earlier parts of mine." Then he says, "I sometimes think that I should have written the *whole* — as a lesson — but it might have proved a lesson to be *learnt* — rather than *avoided* — for passion is a whirl-pool, which is not to be viewed nearly without attraction from its Vortex." Strong stuff, no?' she commented. 'And then he adds, "I must not go on with these reflections, or I shall be letting out some secret or other — to paralyse posterity." Doesn't that sound fishy to you? What causes? What mischief? What paralysing secret?'

The assistant took the book from her and scanned it with interest. 'Do the letters give no insight at all elsewhere?'

'Very little. Of course it's more or less agreed nowadays that it was all tied up with Edleston. The explanation fits, because when Byron took up permanent residence in Cambridge again after his year's absence, Edleston was on the point of leaving. They just had time to say goodbye to one another. So perhaps they were afraid of stirring up a scandal, or perhaps the friendship was too intense and threatening for them to bear. We know, for example, from the poems that Edleston gave Byron a present — a heart made of cornelian, which Byron went and broke later on, as a matter of fact — and we can presume Byron gave him something fairly substantial in return. So they were involved in a sentimental friendship to say the least. But the program won't even admit this outright. I suppose it could have given me some idea of the amount of money he spent on the present, because it's got a lot of stuff on the accounts one way and another, but I didn't dare ask. The whole question seems to upset it terribly. Look here,' and she drew her finger down the page.

WHEN DID YOU FIRST MEET EDLESTON?

OCTOBER 1805.

HOW OLD WAS HE THEN?

TWO YEARS YOUNGER THAN MYSELF TO THE HOUR.

'Seventeen and fifteen,' she said softly to herself. 'Babies!'

WHERE DID YOU MEET HIM?

IF MY MEMORY SERVES ME RIGHTLY, IN TRINITY CHAPEL.

YOUR FRIEND WILLIAM HARNESS SAYS YOU MET HIM IN MORE DRAMATIC CIRCUMSTANCES WHEN YOU SAVED HIM FROM DROWNING. IS THIS FALSE?

IT IS, UNLESS TRINITY CHAPEL IS A BATHING RESORT.

'So far so good,' she said, 'apart from this little bit of tartness. But listen to what comes now.'

WHAT DREW YOU TO HIM?

TO HARNESS OR TO EDLESTON?

TO EDLESTON.

'. . . Now that's easy: it's all in the letters. So it should reply, "His voice first attracted my notice, his countenance fixed it, and his manners attached me to him for ever." Or something like that. Instead it says:

I CANNOT REMEMBER. POSSIBLY, EVEN AT THAT EARLY STAGE, I NOTICED SOMETHING ODD IN HIS PHYSIQUE.

'Which is downright cussed of it. Admittedly Byron had a weak spot for people who were deformed or lame like himself, but Edleston wasn't, as far as we know. Besides it's got plenty more specific information to go on, so why doesn't it use it? And look at *this*!'

WAS THE FRIENDSHIP BETWEEN YOU AND EDLESTON A VERY CLOSE ONE?

VERY CLOSE TO WHAT?

REPHRASE: WAS THE RELATIONSHIP BETWEEN YOU AND EDLESTON AN INTIMATE ONE?

I RESENT THE WORDING, PLEASE REFORMULATE A SECOND
TIME IF YOU WISH ME TO ANSWER.

WHY DO YOU RESENT THE WORDING?

CAZZI MIEI.

'Now I don't quite know what that means, but it
looks pretty cussed again, or else plain rude.'

The assistant consulted the Italian/English dictionary, shut it quickly and blinked. 'It certainly does,' she
said shortly. 'What've we got exactly on this Edleston in
the way of concrete data? I mean how much do we
know about him for certain?'

'Nothing very precise. A few mentions in the letters.
A few records from the university and comments from
fellow students who were there with him. One or two
scribblings in the margins of documents by Byron's
friends and executors when they were going through
his papers — most of them fairly cryptic. No one was
very open about the affair — not even Byron himself.
But Edleston definitely existed all right, and Byron was
definitely very, very fond of him. The letter I quoted
from, the one of July 5th to Elizabeth Pigot, gives the
fullest account: in it Byron states quite clearly that
Edleston was his constant associate at university
(although as a choirboy Edleston probably wouldn't
have been at the university itself, you know, unless he
was studying music and singing in the choir just for the
fun of it), that he loved him more than anyone else in
the world, and that when they were through with their
studies they were thinking of setting up house
together.'

The assistant blinked again, faster. 'Were they now?'
she said in surprise. 'That's not quite what I'd have
expected from England's most famous womanizer. No
wonder the program gets shirty when the subject is
brought up. Perhaps we've gone and tuned the anxiety

parameter for homosexuality too high, then, if what we're dealing with is an out-and-out confessed homosexual.'

'But I don't think he *was* homosexual,' Anna was quick to put in, 'I just think he was muddled. Being surrounded by all those boys at Harrow probably gave a confusing slant to his sex-drives, and the confusion continued at Cambridge. I mean he probably wanted to love somebody — anybody — very badly, and boys were all that there was around. Then, when the girls turned up, he liked them even better, only the first romantic memories stayed connected to the boys. Or something like that.'

'Romantic,' echoed the assistant in distaste, 'you make him sound more like a myopic rapist,' and she withdrew her hand from the terminal where it had been lying. 'Anyway,' she went on, 'whatever he was — homo or pent-up hetero or both — I think we've probably rated the parameter too high; and that's why it can't come clean about the question of the choirboy. This isn't a straightforward research program, remember, it comes close to an emulation of the way Byron's mind worked — or the way we think it might have.' She turned to her colleague, who had just come in, 'Can you remember the rating we gave it — for homosexuality?'

The man raised his eyebrows. 'Tops,' he said. 'The maximum. That was our previous Byron expert, if you remember. He said Byron avoided the subject as a rule, hardly ever mentioned it except to ridicule it, and sprang away like a scalded rabbit on the one or two occasions that anyone male made a pass at him. So we gave him eight out of eight for global anxiety, and only middling for interest as a counterbalance. Why? D'you think it needs redressing?'

The woman scratched her nose thoughtfully with her

70

silver thumbnail. 'Could be. We could try, anyway, and see what happens. It'd be tricky, of course, because anxiety is so closely tied to the other parameters; but, yes, I think all things considered we ought to try and bring it down a little.'

After a brief consultation the two assistants settled themselves at the terminal like a pair of concert pianists, and the woman ran her hands in virtuoso style over the keys. A few minutes later she rose and motioned to Anna to take her place.

'There,' she said, 'that may have done the trick. Go ahead and ask it something else now. We've lowered the anxiety tax to five and put interest up to seven, but only as regards homosexuality in general. This may filter down and affect specific mentions, but it may not. What did you say was the name of the chap who was thought to have assaulted Byron when he was a boy?'

'Lord Grey de Ruthyn.'

'Then let's ask it about him.' And shifting Anna aside once more she typed smartly: WHAT DO YOU FEEL ABOUT LORD GREY DE RUTHYN?

The answer was immediate: HE IS THE MOST DISAGREE- ABLE PERSON THAT EXISTS, MY MOST INVETERATE ENEMY, AND I HAVE BESIDES A PARTICULAR REASON FOR NOT LIKING HIM.

'Oh, you have, have you,' she said, winking at her colleague. WHAT IS THIS REASON?

IT IS SOMETHING BEST KNOWN TO MYSELF.

After a short silence, Anna coughed: 'It doesn't *seem* to have made all that much difference.'

The assistant shrugged and got to her feet. 'No? Well, as I said, maybe it'll take time to filter down. But anyway, I daren't tamper any further than that, or we'll run into conflict with things already stored in the deep memory. Have a go with it now, the way it is. Ask it

71

something more about Cambridge, without mentioning the fascinating Mr What's-he-called by name.'

'But what shall I ask?' Anna wanted to know. She was fairly sure Albè would have been put into a bad mood now from the last question.

The woman shrugged. 'Ask it what you asked before — about what went wrong in Cambridge and why Byron didn't go back there. It's been explained to you often enough; it doesn't really matter *what* you ask it. Just so long as you keep a weather eye on the language it uses and make sure it doesn't jar.'

Anna set to work. As the new answers came through, however, she began to see that something in the language *had* changed. It didn't jar exactly, but — she couldn't quite put her finger on it — it was in a different key somehow. Yes, that's what it was. The language was in a subtly different key.

7   Memoirs and Mementos

―――――――

Oho, if things had changed! They were still changing. He lay carefully poised on the bed in his best damask dressing-gown, as laundered, spruced and perfumed as a well-schooled whore and with scarcely more claim to dignity, and debated within himself on what he was about to do. The mattress had a slope to it, and in spite of the occasional effort to remain in its middle, he could feel himself willy-nilly slipping gradually floorwards: a state of affairs which he couldn't help thinking rather appropriate. He *was* slipping, there was no doubt about it; and in more ways than one. Admittedly he hadn't wanted to. Admittedly he had been pushed. But by now he was definitely slipping – and at a tidy pace, too – along a plane which was steep enough and smooth enough for there to be no way left of slowing his progress or turning aside. Where the plane led he did not know; all he knew was that it led down, down, down, and that in the dizziness of the descent he was agog to get to the bottom. (A clumsy way of putting it, he thought to himself with a chuckle, but never mind.) Partner in the debate, mostly listening but sometimes voicing snide objections of his own in a strong Scottish accent, was the Rev. George Gordon – his Calvinist conscience. It was the Rev. George, in point of fact, who had introduced the downwards metaphor. For nothing ever went up for that high-minded gentleman; everything went down, and preferably into darkness while it was about it. Not that he could have appreciated the irony in the last part of the phrasing, though, since there were certain things that it didn't do to tell the old fogey at all, and others which, even if you did tell him, he would be at a loss to understand. He had no sense of fun whatever.

'Ah yes, but the push was a very gentle one,' was the next cavil the Rev. came up with, 'if push it was. And you didn't put up much resistance to it, either, did you now? *Did* you?'

He shook his head to silence the voice. What it said was unfair. Gentle or not, it was Edleston who had done the pushing. For himself, he'd have been perfectly content to let things stand as they were. Except in dreamy moments when his fancy was on a light rein and could gallop ahead unchecked into wilder territory (or in drunken ones, which came to much the same thing), he had never asked for more on his own account than that he and Edleston should go on, day after lazy day, doing the things they already did: spending their time together, sharing their amusements and the odd lapses into boredom, reading, scribbling, catching hold of whatever the hours had to offer, and wandering in each other's company through the humdrum paths of everyday college life. It hadn't seemed wrong so much as impolitic to want for more.

Not he but Edleston − the dry, demure Edleston, so self-contained, so chary of letting others see what was going on behind that smooth marble forehead of his − had made the first move; not he but Edleston had seen fit to put a stop to the humdrum. And now that the stop had been placed − or now that at least a comma had − then what harm could there be, he wondered, in adding a bit of punctuation of his own? What could be wrong in opening a parenthesis, for example, or winding up with a rousing exclamation mark?

'Whoa there! Steady. It was only a trinket the lad gave you,' pointed out the Rev. George stolidly; he never went in for finesse or originality in his speech. 'Aren't you putting two and two together to make five?'

Which was unfair too. He could allow that a cornelian was no great shakes as far as jewellery was concerned, but to someone of Edleston's background the cost would seem high and had probably eaten up a considerable part of his allowance. The cornelian was in the shape of a heart, too. Didn't that speak clear enough? And what was more, when he had made him the present, not only had Edleston gone bright pink in the face and stood staring at the ground in silence for quite some time before summoning up the courage to show it to him, but he had even shed a tear on the cornelian before parting with it for, thinking back on it, the stone had been damp when it reached his own hand.

'Fellow had a bad cold at the time. One of his stinkers,' commented the Rev. G., unmoved. 'He's never mentioned the matter again, either, and he's done his level best to avoid being left alone in your company ever since. That's not much of a push to my way of thinking. To me it looks more as if he's regretting what he's done and wants to undo it; as if the lad isn't pushing but pulling away. Not that I blame him,' he added a little smugly. 'First you encourage him, then when he responds — and it was a very pretty gesture of his I thought, and I can't for the life of me see why you made all that fuss about it — you take fright and bolt to London, dragging me along with you to that . . . that . . .', here words seemed to fail him for a moment, 'that . . . infamous establishment, on the excuse you had to "prove your manhood" or however it was you put it. Prove your manhood, stuff and nonsense! Prove your beasthood is more like it. Then tears and recriminations, and shilly-shally, shuffle-shuffle, and you start scribbling verses and wasting time instead of going back to your studies. And then suddenly about-face again and off you go to the moneylenders and the jewellers (two other establishments you would do well to keep clear of in the future, I may add), and come rushing back here again to take up with that poor little mite of a choirboy again as if nothing had happened. No wonder he's been acting cold towards you: he doesn't know where he stands — on his head or on his heels. And the same goes for you.'

Here of course the Reverend had a point. Since his return Edleston had in fact been acting very coldly towards him indeed. Not only had he turned down the invitation to resume their early-morning rides on the excuse that it was bad for his voice to breathe all that frosty air before service, but he had refused steadfastly to come swimming. For three evenings running he had avoided the usual gathering of cronies and had sent a pipsqueak of an errand boy in his stead with a written message to say that he was studying (studying what, for goodness' sake? No one in their senses studied for a paltry degree in music), and on the few occasions when he had put in an appearance he had sat apart from the others, offhand, irritable, and alert as a hare to scuttle off at the first opportunity. Long too had noticed something was amiss. 'What's got into our young Master Ed?' he'd asked, half joking, half genuinely offended. 'You'd think we smelt, the way he's carrying on. Well, if so, I don't think it's you, Byron, and it ain't me for sure, so I'm afraid it must be Bankes and these awesome feet of his.' And absent-mindedly he had emptied his glass of claret down Bankes's boot.

But — snuffs to the Reverend — he didn't think himself that this cold behaviour of Edleston's meant that the boy was pulling away; merely that he was shy and bewildered. More likely, shaken by the result of the first move he had made and afraid of making another, the poor fellow was now waiting in miserable suspense for a sign of encouragement from the other side — a sign which, being underneath the bravado every bit as shy and bewildered himself, he had not yet dared to give.

For the tenth, perhaps the twentieth, time that afternoon his hand strayed to his dressing-gown pocket, and he fingered nervously the blue satin box which he had been carrying around with him now for the best part of the week. In it, on a cushion of darker blue velvet, lay the object with which he intended to bolster his young friend's punctuation for him (and it darn well ought to, too, he thought respectfully: it had cost him a packet); the sign, unless he was very much mistaken for which Edleston was waiting. He drew out the box, blinked at the contents, and put it back in his pocket again. But not before the Reverend George had taken due note. 'It don't seem right to me to give a costly present like that in exchange for a mere cornelian,' he barked severely. 'Very good, you are older and wealthier and of higher birth, and it may well be your duty to show yourself open-handed. We've been into this before. You want the best for your friend, want to impress him, win him round. Very good. Very good. You also want to leave him a reminder that'll last him a lifetime and come in handy if ever he gets into a financial fix. But all the same, don't you think you may be overshooting the mark a bit with this . . . this vulgar great gewgaw here? Where do you think it'll lead you, this bright stone with its murky message? I'd tell you myself, if only you'd stop twittering and listen for a moment: it'll plummet you down, the pair of you, into dark regions where neither of you will feel at home, and from which neither of you — green as you are — will be able to find the exit. That's where it'll lead you both, mark my words: into the abyss.'

Descent and darkness again — the favourite metaphors. Plummeting and perdition. Worming himself resolutely back to the middle of the bed, and shutting his ears against his conscience's dour predictions, he draped the folds of his dressing-gown into place once more to hide the slight bulge of his stomach, tucked his gammy foot well out of sight, consulted his watch and took a last look around him to make sure that the scene was set exactly as he wished it.

Let him see now. Boyce had been given the afternoon off, the dogs had been fed and banished to the stables for the time being. So far so good. The next-door room was fairly tidy — at least tidier than usual, while his writing table had been left in a state of deliberate muddle, so as to make it appear he had been working and had interrupted his writing for a moment to take a chance rest. He had strewn a few books on the bed, too, so that it would seem natural to invite Edleston to sit down on it at some point with a, 'Take a look at this jackass Southey, how slipshod his rhyme is here,' or, perhaps more in keeping with the mood, 'Take a look at this couplet of Pope's, how sublime the phrasing is'; and he had remembered to leave the door to the staircase ajar. Perfect. Just as it should be: everything so contrived that Edleston — provided he arrived before the mattress had disgorged its burden on to the floor once and for all — could walk straight in and come upon him reclining in this intimate and (he very much hoped) alluring position. Yes, everything was in readiness; now he had only to wait.

He put his watch to his ear to make sure it was working. It was. Or at least, however slowly it was going, it hadn't actually stopped. He gave it a shake and listened again. 'Och!' came the voice of the Reverend George from somewhere inside him, growling above the ticking, 'it smacks of downright corruption, if you ask me: all these preparations and what not. Poor little beggar. If only you'd stop for a second before it's too late and consider . . .'

But now there seemed to be another voice, louder, more cheerful, more compelling, whispering excitedly at the same time, 'Don't think. Just go ahead and give it to him. If he accepts he is hooked. If he refuses there's no harm done; but if he accepts he is hooked.' He could hardly be bothered to listen to the Reverend George. And when above the babble, he heard the sound of feet bounding up the stairway outside, and a light but clearly audible rap on the door, both inner voices were silenced on the instant, and he was aware instead of the sound of his own public one calling out unevenly and at an unusually high pitch, 'Is that you, Edleston? The door's open. Give it a kick and come along in. In here, I mean — in the bedroom.'

The door swung slowly inwards and Edleston, his chorister's surplice wrapped round his neck like a scarf, stood hesitantly on the threshold. The choirboy stood only two inches taller than he when they were on a level, but in the present arrangement the impression he gave was that of an arch-angel visiting a worm. 'What's the matter, Byron? You down with the grippe too?' he enquired politely, covering his nose with the hem of the surplice and lodging himself firmly in the doorway.

79

'Do you need anything? Was that why you sent for me? And how is it Boyce has deserted you like this, leaving everything upside down and the door open?'

'Oh darn. Has he? Did he?' he asked vaguely, running a hand through his hair to add the finishing touch to his creative disarray. 'Too bad. Never mind. Come in. Take a seat. And take that muffler from your face; there's nothing wrong with me. I've been writing hard, as you can see, and now I'm resting.'

'From the onslaughts of the muse?'

'From the onslaughts of the muse. Precisely. Is there anything wrong with that?'

Edleston buried his chin in his surplice again and shrugged. 'Nothing,' he said on a slightly wobbly note, 'nothing. Only you looked so stricken I thought you must be ill. Grippe, or a stomach upset or something.' He edged nervously towards the bed and then, spotting a chair on the far side of the room, made for it hastily, and sweeping the clothes that were piled on it summarily on to the floor, drew it alongside the bed and sat down on it with a thump.

As on their last meeting, the boy's resemblance to a hare was striking: the watchfulness, the upright, quivering carriage, and the eyes darting, now to the floor, now to the window, and then coming to rest in between in a kind of pained fascination on the bed and the folds of the dressing-gown.

There was a long, uneasy silence. Funnily enough, now that Edleston was doing enough quivering for both of them, he found that his own had stopped. Indeed there was no more reason for nervousness, for he could tell just by looking at the boy's profile, just by feeling the shaking of the two spindly knees as they brushed against the bed cover, that the Reverend George had been wrong and he had been right: the

80

coolness of the past week had been due to fright alone. Edleston was his now for the taking. He had only to stretch out and touch him (and if he waited a few minutes longer and let the mattress do its work there would be no need even to stretch), and the rest would come as soon and as easily as he wanted: the bed was there (it never had been before), there was no one to disturb them or come between them (as there nearly always had been), the atmosphere was so charged by now with their respective vibrations that some kind of report or explosion was more or less guaranteed to follow on the smallest of sparks, and, amazingly enough, not only was his conscience silent for once in a while — stunned, like as not, by the sheer horror of the events it was called to witness — but his flesh, which had always blandly refused to stir itself for anything male, however young, however winning, seemed to be having second thoughts. Loud, outspoken, eloquent thoughts; very pleasurable ones.

Putting a hand to his neck he undid another button of his shirt and drew forth the cornelian. Edleston's knees jerked together: 'You're wearing it!' he said incredulously. 'You're not angry then. When you stayed away like that for so long I thought you must be. And then you came back and said nothing. So when I got your message, I didn't know what to think. In fact, when I poked my head round the door I was half expecting you to throw the thing back in my face.'

'Angry?' he said softly. 'Angry? How could I be angry? Have I ever been angry with you that you recall?'

The boy's eyes met his own for a second, sending a hot, sweet lump to the back of his throat as if he had swallowed a piece of honeycomb and it had stuck there. 'No, Byron,' he replied, he too swallowing as if he had a lump to deal with. 'Short-tempered once or twice maybe; never angry. But then . . .' and he shut his eyes tightly and took a deep breath, '. . . I've never done anything so stupid before. I don't know what came over me to take a step like that. I feel such a blundering ass.'

The way this was said was so open and so simple, and the speaker himself so appealing, sitting there with his eyelashes trembling on his flushed cheek like the wings of a pair of dark velvet butterflies, that tenderness for Edleston overwhelmed him of a sudden, and without waiting for the slope to account for the last four or five inches or so that still divided them, he reached out on impulse for his friend's arm and pulled it gently towards him. Nor did he let up until, unresisting, the slim body followed the arm and toppled on to the bed, where it lay splayed across his own fatter one like a crossbar.

There was another moment's silence and stillness before Edleston gasped and began to roll himself further down the bed. Then came a brief struggle as the boy – by far the weaker of the two – tried to break free of the grasp that held him. Books flew, noses snorted, limbs grappled, and – although he never admitted this to Edleston, neither then nor later – deep down inside him a great burst of laughter rang out, for the sheer joy of the combat.

He thought quickly, as wrestling practice had taught him to do. Using feet instead of hands, so intent on keeping his hold as to not to give a damn at this point whether Edleston noticed his foot or not, he scissored him neatly, pinned him down with all the strength he could muster and, his hands now free, delved into the pocket of his own dressing-gown for the famous box. If he waited a hundred years, he could scarcely hope for a better moment than this, he thought to himself in elation. Hang the Reverend George. Hang the moralists. And hang prudence and caution along with them: he wasn't going to consider strategy or seemliness any longer; this was the moment to act.

Edleston, who had stopped struggling, watched saucer-eyed as the box was produced, took it from him gingerly and, without opening it, balanced it on the end of his long, bony nose. 'For me?' he asked wonderingly, when he had got his breath back.

'For you. Open it. Please.'

'Not yet. Let me just enjoy the feel of it first.' The long, thin nose twitched. 'It's heavy for a start.'

'It is.'

'And it's beautiful.'

'You can't tell that with your nose.'

'I can. I can tell a lot more than you'd think. For example I can tell it's expensive, because it smells expensive.'

'Mmm,' he agreed smilingly, 'you're right there and no mistake.' No sooner had he said this, however, than he realized he had trodden on delicate ground here — and with the grace of an elephant.

Edleston's nose crinkled and the box slipped on to the coverlet with a light thud: 'Then I shan't be able to accept it,' he said sadly. 'You've spent so much on me already. The horse . . . the books . . . that velvet jacket that's on order with the tailor . . . I've put you to trouble enough as it is. And then there's my aunt to be considered. Certain things I can explain away. This . . .' and he turned his head sideways and gave the box a poke with his finger, '. . . this not even she would swallow.'

'I sincerely hope not, poor creature,' he said lightly, cursing himself for his clumsiness. 'Nobody's asking her to do anything so heroic. This is a secret gift, to be worn next to the skin, as I wear yours. Neither she nor anyone else need ever know of its existence. You can't decide till you open it, anyway. Open it. Go ahead. See what's inside.'

Slowly Edleston prised himself free of the legs encircling his waist, sat up, and took the box in his hands.

'Open it. Please. I beg of you,' he entreated him.

Very slowly Edleston opened the box and, so still now that he seemed scarcely to be breathing, sat looking at the jewel in silence. The moment was again one of extreme delicacy: thump, thump, thump went the elephant, its feet under severe check this time, and thump, thump, thump went the heart inside it. 'Could you accept it, do you think?' he asked Edleston trepidatingly. 'Keep it and wear it for myself and yourself alone to see, in the name of friendship?'

'In the name of friendship?' Edleston echoed in a whisper. 'In the name of *friendship*?' he repeated dazedly, turning towards him with a look of total bewilderment. 'Why? Is this the gift of a friend?'

The question brought a flush to his face, and he avoided the boy's eyes and was silent a moment before answering. For he must be honest with himself. Until now he had tacitly assumed — and not only for the Reverend's benefit — that friendship was at least one of his motives in making the gift. Complicated by others if you like. Tainted by others if you prefer. But it had certainly been present amongst them, or so he had assumed. Now, however, he was no longer sure. For even in the abstract, for mere purposes of discussion, it was hardly correct to speak of friendship, surely, when the chief emotion that the so-called friend's company aroused in you was an overriding desire to penetrate his body with a hard and pungent part of your own

84

(which alas, was all he felt like doing now; and not at all in the abstract). Take anything of which you were fond — a beautiful painting, for example; would you go and ram a rolling-pin through it to show your appreciation? Certainly not. No more than you would spear your best horse, impale your dog, bore holes through your favourite pair of boots, or welcome an eagerly awaited guest by stubbing a walking stick through his navel. So to be quite honest, friendship didn't come into it at all.

He looked up again, and Edleston's image floated towards him blurrily now, through what might have been a haze of tears but could equally well have been embarrassment or sheer animal lust. 'No,' he admitted huskily, hardly able to pronounce his words (though for all the tears or the embarrassment or whatever, his enjoyment of the situation was so acute that he still felt himself on the verge of bursting out laughing). 'No. It's not friendship. You know it isn't.' And then, more huskily still, 'What is it with you?'

The answer was not quite what he had expected. Edleston shrugged, and picking himself off the bed limb by limb he rose to his full height, carefully unwound the surplice (part of which had unwound itself already during the tussle) from around his neck, and still very neatly and methodically laid it on the chair. Then he stooped down towards the bed, took the jewel from its nest of velvet and twisting his hair into a knot at the back to keep it out of the way, hung it round his bare throat and clasped the chain shut.

'With me,' he said simply, shaking his hair free and giving a shy but very sweet smile, 'it is love. Only my case, of course, is rather different. You'll soon see why.'

8　More Memory Jogging

'It's the end part particularly I'm worried about,' Anna complained to the female assistant as they inspected the fresh material together. 'That fiddling you did with the anxiety index seems to have thrown things a bit squiffy. Listen, and see what you think.' And she began to read aloud the latest dialogue, alternating her normal voice for her own contributions, with a lower, gruffer one for LB's more lordly and Byronic answers.

'ALBÈ, WHAT HAPPENED TO PREVENT YOU FROM RETURNING TO CAMBRIDGE FOR THE LENT TERM 1806?

I WAS NOT PREVENTED FROM RETURNING TO CAMBRIDGE, I DID NOT CHOOSE TO RETURN THERE.

WHY DID YOU CHOOSE TO RETURN SO LATE, THEN?

I TAKE IT YOU ARE STILL REFERRING TO THE UNIVERSITY. AS A MEMBER OF THE NOBILITY, I COULD RETURN WHEN I LIKED.

WEREN'T YOU A STUDENT, THOUGH, AS WELL AS A NOBLE?

I WAS. BUT I WAS FIRST AND FOREMOST A NOBLE.

COULD YOU EXPLAIN, PLEASE.

WILLINGLY. FOR NOBLES, SUCH AS MYSELF, AND ELDEST SONS OF NOBLES, THE RULES OF RESIDENCE WERE WAIVED, AS WAS ALSO COMPULSORY ATTENDANCE AT CHAPEL. WE HAD NO EXAMINATIONS TO BOTHER OURSELVES ABOUT EITHER, NO STUDY UNLESS WE FELT LIKE IT. WE COULD DRESS AS WE SAW FIT, EXCEPT FOR MEAL TIMES WHEN BREECHES AND WHITE SILK STOCKINGS WERE THE THING, AND WE HAD FIRST CUT OF THE ROAST AT DINNER IN HALL. FORTUNATELY FOR

OUR STOCKINGS. LATER EATERS WERE FACED WITH A BOARD AS GORY AS A BATTLEFIELD. IS THAT SUFFICIENT?

YES, THANK YOU.

'Now the bit about meals intrigued me,' she said, interrupting her reading to explain this to the assistant, 'as it seemed to contradict another thing it had said earlier — about living expenses being so exorbitant, and being out of pocket on that account, and so on; so I asked it:

WHY WERE YOUR LIVING EXPENSES SO HIGH, IF YOU ATE IN COLLEGE?

I DIDN'T EAT THERE OFTEN. IT WAS NOT CONSIDERED FASHIONABLE TO DO SO. BUT THEY RAN THE PLACE LIKE A HOSTEL, AND A D———D EXPENSIVE ONE TOO. (By the way,' she added, 'the "damned" with a dash is in order, but I don't think Byron would have used the word "fashionable" in that context. It sounds far too recent somehow.) IF YOU ATE THERE YOU PAID. IF YOU DIDN'T EAT THERE YOU PAID. AND IF YOU ATE IN YOUR CHAMBERS YOU PAID THE KITCHEN SEPARATELY, I.E. TWICE OVER, AND USUALLY TWICE AS MUCH AS THE GOODS COST IN THE MARKET. YOU ALSO PAID TO BE LET OFF CHAPEL.

BUT YOU SAID YOU WERE EXEMPTED FROM CHAPEL SERVICES.

INDEED I WAS. BUT IT MADE NO DIFFERENCE TO THE ACCOUNTS. I STILL HAD TO PAY THROUGH THE NOSE.'

The assistant, who had followed all this with a look of growing complacency, shook her head. 'It's not a *bit* squiffy, Anna,' she stated, a trifle warmly, 'it's working beautifully. Just look at that language. I don't know if you can appreciate it to the full, but the reply I DIDN'T EAT THERE OFTEN, just to take one instance, is a linguistic triumph in its way. Not only does the program immediately cotton on to the connection between number of meals and cost, but it realizes that it can use it as an answer without spelling out any of the details. See how it uses "there", too — the same way as you did; not mentioning the place, but taking it for granted that it is the last place mentioned. For a human speaker, a short-cut like that is too obvious to be worth mentioning, but for a program it's real sophistication. Can't you see how beautifully naturally these answers read?'

Anna chewed her lip and frowned. 'Well, yes, I suppose they do,' she agreed, 'but it was the *character* that I meant when I said it had gone squiffy, not the grammar or the syntax or what-have-you. I'll go on to the next bit and you'll see what I mean. Where had I got to?'

'Money,' said the assistant.

'Ah, yes. Money. Well, since we'd got on to the subject and it seemed to be chatting away about it quite freely for a change, I asked: WAS THAT WHY YOU RAN INTO DEBT? But I must have been a bit too blunt because instead of answering me, it hedged with a: QUESTION INCOMPLETE. PLEASE REFORMULATE.'

'Which is not hedging, Anna,' the assistant put in. 'It was right; your question was far too elliptical.'

'But you said just now it could handle "theres" and "thats",' Anna objected.

'Yes, but not when the "that" harks back to something mentioned four questions earlier, as in this case. It's asking too much. Anyway. So you reformulated the question?'

'Yes. I asked: WERE YOU UNABLE TO MEET YOUR COLLEGE EXPENSES IN CAMBRIDGE? and it said: I DON'T KNOW WHAT YOU MEAN BY THAT. I WAS UNABLE TO MEET ANY MONEY-LENDERS IN CAMBRIDGE.

WHY DID YOU WANT TO MEET MONEY-LENDERS? I asked. BECAUSE THEY ARE NOTORIOUSLY CHARMING PEOPLE.'

The assistant held up her hand. 'Aha,' she said, '*now*

I see what you mean. Yes, there's something definitely squiffy there.' And she polished her glasses briskly and peered at the print-out. 'Yes, you're right. Why on earth should it say that money-lenders are charming? Unless, of course,' she added after a moment's thought, 'Byron himself had a soft spot for the category. Did he, that you know?'

Anna laughed. 'Oh, no,' she said lightly, 'but don't worry about that part. It's only joking. That's quite in character. The *un*characteristic bit I mentioned comes a little later on.'

'Joking?' The assistant shut her eyes and muttered something under her breath to check her impatience. 'For God's sake, Anna,' she let out with a sigh, 'I've got high hopes in the program's performance myself, as well you know, but — get this straight in your mind — it can't *joke*. If it asserts that money-lenders are charming, it's because this information is stored inside it somewhere. And if the information is wrong and doesn't represent Byron's views faithfully, then it must be located and corrected. But that is something we can deal with later,' she added more kindly. 'Go ahead. It's lucky you discovered it.'

'Well, to me it was joking,' Anna insisted, 'at least I thought it was, so I told it . . . and she went back to the voices of her dialogue:

'PLEASE BE SERIOUS, ALBÈ.

PLEASE BE SERIOUS YOURSELF, ANNA.

YOU NEEDED MONEY.

I NEEDED MONEY.

HOW MUCH MONEY?

THAT IS AN INDELICATE QUESTION. SUFFICE IT TO SAY THAT I NEEDED A LARGE SUM OF MONEY.

SORRY ABOUT THAT. WHY DID YOU NEED TO RAISE SUCH A LARGE SUM OF MONEY?

WHAT ARE YOU SORRY ABOUT?

ABOUT ASKING AN INDELICATE QUESTION.

THEN WHY DID YOU ASK A SECOND ONE?

BECAUSE I WANT TO KNOW THE ANSWER.

FAIR ENOUGH. WOULD YOU BE SO GOOD AS TO REPEAT THE QUESTION?

WHY DID YOU NEED TO RAISE SUCH A LARGE SUM OF MONEY?

'It took some time over this one,' she explained to the assistant, riffling through her notes, 'and then in the end it didn't really answer but sort of got round it by saying:

YOU KNOW, ANNA, THAT'S A QUESTION MY MOTHER OFTEN USED TO ASK. So then I asked: WHAT ANSWER DID YOU GIVE YOUR MOTHER? to try and pin it down.

I SUGGESTED SHE REFER TO MY TUTOR. It said: MOST OF THE BILLS WENT THROUGH HIM. IF YOU ARE INTERESTED I SUGGEST YOU DO THE SAME.

'Monkeying about as usual,' she said fondly, shaking her head and earning herself another glare of impatience from the assistant. 'But wait for it now. This is where I took the plunge, and this is where the oddness starts.

YOU MENTIONED THAT PART OF YOUR ALLOWANCE WENT ON GIFTS. DID YOU MAKE ANY PARTICULARLY EXPENSIVE ONES AT THAT TIME?

AT WHAT TIME?

DURING THE OCTOBER TERM OF 1805.

'Now *this*', she explained again from her notes for the assistant's benefit, 'kept it busy for ages. Eventually it said:

IT IS PROBABLE THAT I DID SO.

HOW PROBABLE? I asked.

DO YOU WISH FOR A PRECISE NUMERIC GRADING?

NO, JUST A VAGUE IDEA.

I PRESUME YOUR REQUEST TO BE FOR AN ORIENTATIVE GRADING IN NATURAL LANGUAGE. THE ANSWER IS: HIGHLY.

'Very computerish here, of course, and very stiff,' she added aside. 'So: WERE THESE GIFTS MADE TO YOUR FRIEND, JOHN EDLESTON? I went on.'

ARE YOU ACQUAINTED WITH MR EDLESTON?

NO.

THEN IT IS FORWARD OF YOU TO USE HIS CHRISTIAN NAME. PLEASE REFORMULATE YOUR QUESTION.

'Stiffer still!' she said with a laugh. 'But anyway reformulate I did.

WERE THESE GIFTS MADE TO YOUR FRIEND MR JOHN EDLESTON?

IT IS PROBABLE THAT THEY WERE.

HOW PROBABLE? I asked.

Now it chewed on this for quite a while too,' she said thoughtfully, 'and then, after a few flashes and blinks, it said:

MERELY PROBABLE. DATA INSUFFICIENT TO GRADE HYPOTHESIS.

YOU MUST HAVE BEEN VERY FOND OF HIM.

"MUST" IMPLIES NECESSITY, NOT PROBABILITY. I WAS PROBABLY VERY FOND OF HIM.

COULD THIS FONDNESS OF YOURS FOR MR EDLESTON HAVE BEEN ONE OF YOUR MAIN REASONS FOR NOT RETURNING TO CAMBRIDGE THAT FOLLOWING FEBRUARY?

OF COURSE IT COULD. MUST I REMIND YOU THAT POSSIBILITY IS A WEAKER NOTION THAN PROBABILITY?'

She paused. 'Well, by this time I was getting a bit fed up with all this dotting of i's and crossing of t's,' she confessed. 'Byron himself would never have been so finickerty, you know.' She glanced briefly at the assistant's profile, 'I suppose there's nothing much you can do about that, though, is there? About the finickertiness, I mean?'

91

'No,' said the assistant shortly, 'because it's not being finickerty; it's being logical.' She glared at the younger woman over the rims of her glasses. 'Funnily enough there hasn't been much demand for illogical programs to date.'

'Oh,' answered Anna contritely, 'I didn't realize that. Anyway, I'm afraid I *was* losing patience a little by this stage, so I gave it a dose of its own medicine and said:

NO, THERE IS NO NECESSITY FOR YOU TO REMIND ME OF ANYTHING OF THE KIND.

HA, it went. And then: I SHALL VERY PROBABLY REMEM-BER THAT.'

She turned laughingly towards the assistant, 'So you see, it *has* got a sense of humour. But I wasn't going to let myself get side-tracked yet again, and I went on and asked it:

WAS THIS FONDNESS FOR MR EDLESTON ONE OF YOUR MAIN REASONS FOR NOT RETURNING TO CAMBRIDGE THE FOLLOWING FEBRUARY?'

'Hmm. Let's see,' grunted the assistant, and briefly consulting the dial of her wristwatch she seized hold of the print-out and began to read aloud the dialogue herself. Unlike Anna, she read rapidly, making no attempt to distinguish between voices, but using a flat, businesslike tone for the entire exchange:

'NO IT WAS NOT ONE OF MY MAIN REASONS, WHY DO YOU ASK?

BECAUSE I THINK YOU WERE DEEPLY INVOLVED WITH HIM EMOTIONALLY. WERE YOU?

WAS I WHAT?

INVOLVED WITH EDLESTON EMOTIONALLY?

VERB MISSING?

WERE YOU INVOLVED WITH EDLESTON EMOTIONALLY?

I THINK NOT. I INDULGED IN MANY SENTIMENTAL FRIENDSHIPS WITH YOUNG AND PRETTY MEMBERS OF MY OWN

92

SEX WHILE AT HARROW. THE FRIENDSHIP WITH EDLESTON WAS MERELY ANOTHER SUCH.

DIDN'T THE HOMOSEXUAL IMPLICATIONS OF IT BOTHER YOU?

LORD NO. NOT A BIT. I HAVE RATHER A PENCHANT FOR SODOMY ONE WAY AND ANOTHER. I ONCE PLANNED EVEN TO WRITE A STUDY ENTITLED 'PEDERASTY PROVED TO BE PRAISE-WORTHY FROM ANCIENT AUTHORS AND MODERN PRACTICE'.

SO THE SUBJECT WAS NOT ONE YOU FOUND OFFENSIVE?

EVIDENTLY NOT. I SEE NO HARM IN PUTTING IT ABOUT IN WHATEVER PLACE A MAN PLEASES, PROVIDED IT PLEASES HIM, THAT IS, AND THE PLACE TAKES IT IN GOOD PART. WHAT DO YOU THINK?'

With this the woman rolled up the paper and grunted again. 'A far cry from Lord Grey de Whatsit,' she commented with raised eyebrows. 'Is that all there is?'

'On the printer, yes,' said Anna, 'but there's one more question I asked it — with the printer switched off this time, because it was a delicate one. Having got so far, you see, I thought I might just as well go the whole hog, and so I asked it point blank:

DID YOU PRACTISE IT YOURSELF?'

'Oho,' said the assistant, giving another lightning wipe to her glasses and peering at Anna's notebook, 'and what did it have to say to that?'

Anna withdrew the notebook and smiled. 'Something rather mysterious and rather sweet, I thought,' she said with a trace of wistfulness. 'It said: HAD I PRACTISED, ANNA DEAR, I SHOULD HAVE BEEN A MORE CONSUMMATE PERFORMER. It's never called me "dear" before,' she explained, 'it's the very first time.'

The assistant made no comment on this but went back to scanning the print-out. 'Uneven,' she said with a frown, speaking more to herself than to the girl beside her. 'Formal and then confidential within the space of seconds. Blast! Perhaps we have gone and overdone things a bit. I wonder. It uses the oddest expressions too.' She glanced up sharply. 'What do you suppose it means exactly,' she asked, 'by "putting it about"? It's a figure of speech I don't think I've heard before.' Anna examined her cuticles. 'Well, perhaps it's not so hard to understand once you've grasped what "it" stands for,' she said without looking up. 'The phrase is one Byron borrowed from the famous boxer, John "Gentleman" Jackson. But it only crops up once, as far as I can remember, in one of Byron's raciest letters. It's not a characteristic expression of his at all — especially not when talking to a woman, and to one he doesn't even know very well. Because "it", you see, was . . .'

The assistant interrupted her hurriedly. 'Quite, quite,' she said in a cross tone of voice, 'then we must shove it back up again. I mean,' she corrected herself more crossly still, 'we must put the anxiety values for homosexuality back where they were before. I'm inclined to agree with you, Anna; the balance has been seriously disturbed. The program can't possibly be made available to its sponsors — not even to a well-disposed clique of Byron enthusiasts — in its present state.' And rolling up her sleeves she addressed herself to the terminal once more and began tinkering with the keys.

'Keep still,' she said, placing a hand on Anna's stool. 'Wait. When I've finished you can go back and ask it about Cambridge again, so we can compare answers and see whether it's better this way or worse.'

'Oh dear, I'd rather not ask it *exactly* the same questions,' Anna objected. 'It doesn't like repetition. So if you don't mind, when I go back I'll ask it something similar, but a little bit different. I hope it goes back to exactly how it was before,' she added. 'I liked it better that way.'

9   More Memoirs

ALBÈ, FROM SUMMER 1806 TO SUMMER 1807 YOU WERE ONCE
MORE ABSENT FROM CAMBRIDGE. WHY WAS THIS?
Cambridge again? The perseverance of bulldogs
these questioners of his. Not that he could blame them,
he supposed, when they had picked on such a very
interesting subject. But since the full answer to that
question, and the full story behind it, was something
that he had never told to any living man or woman
(unless he'd let fall one or two hints of it to Shelley that
night in Ravenna, when they'd sat up till five in the
morning confessing to one another their wicked ways;
which he might well have done, come to think of it, but
couldn't really remember), he most certainly didn't
intend to make it public now. The less said about it all,
the better.

The turning point, of course, had come . . .

Wait a second, though; he'd better make sure first
that the secret *was* still safe. For what if he *had* told it to
Shelley, and Shelley had passed it on to Mrs Shelley?
Mightn't Mrs Shelley then have passed it on to someone else, or even put it in a novel? Lady novelists were
a scurvy breed. Let him see now: Shelley. Shelley.
Shelley, Percy B. . . . Shelley, Mary − vide: Godwin,
Mary . . . Godwin . . . Godwin . . . No, thank goodness;
even if he had told Shelley, and even if Shelley had let
his wife in on the secret, from what he could tell it

96

would seem that the lady had been as restrained and upright in her writings as he remembered her to have been in her neat little carriage. Good girl. And Augusta? *She* knew well enough, of course, but everything was safe with Augusta. How then about the madcap Lamb, who had once hinted to him narkily that she had got wind of the affair? (Although who she could have had it from was a mystery. *What* was it she had hissed at him so charmingly at their last meeting? 'I could BREAK you, Byron. One word from me about a certain little incident in your Cambridge past, and I could have you hounded out of every drawing-room in Europe!' Something like that.) Had she gossiped? Better check. Lamb . . . Lamb, C. . . . Lamb, G. . . . Lamb, W., Viscount Melbourne . . . (Good gracious! William Lamb, Prime Minister of England? Glad he hadn't lived to see that!) . . . No, as far as he could make out, the Lamb, although at the opposite pole to Mary Shelley and just about as restrained and upright as a boa constrictor, also seemed to have kept her peace on that particular topic. So perhaps she too had felt herself bound by a peculiar code of loyalty in the end, or else she had merely been bluffing.

The turning point, anyway, had come right there, with that confounded present. He'd never been a good giver of presents – not even later in life when he should have known better. He over-gave. Pieces of himself stuck to his gifts and tainted them with something that could easily pass (and nearly always did) for meanness and prodigality at the same time but never generosity. For he loved giving, and hated receiving, and no man thus put together ever made a graceful donor. His gifts were heavy and were meant to be so. And this one was no exception. Quite apart from its sentimental weight, it had weighed so hard on his purse that a full decade later, when the recipient was no longer there to wear it and he, the giver, could no longer remember who he'd bought it from and what had been the colour of the stone, he had still been paying for it — or at any rate still trying to clear himself of the debt he had incurred to raise the original purchase money. So, whatever the mineral was, it had been a downright millstone that way.

And what was more, just as the Reverend George had predicted — direction and all — like a millstone it had weighed on his conscience. Most of the biographers, he could see, didn't seem to have grasped this side of the question fully; they seemed to take it as a simple matter of fact that he'd been prone from the start to what they breezily dismissed as 'sentimental friendships' with young and pretty members of his own sex. (Which was true, of course, but only up to a point. He had always liked having beautiful things around him — animate or inanimate, male *or* female. He'd always liked taking care of them too; whether this meant, in the case of a painting, having it well framed or hung, or in the case of a protégé at school slipping the odd five-pound note into his hand or buying him a cravat or a becoming new haircut. It was a form of investment, if you like, or a generic form of gratitude towards beauty itself. But sentiment — the way these learned ladies and gentlemen evidently meant it — hadn't come into it at all: he had not, emphatically *not*, been in the habit of mooning over little boys.) To the biographers, therefore, the Edleston affair — or what little they knew about it — didn't pose much of a problem, and they could put it down every whit as breezily as just another of these friendships of his — a little more disturbing maybe, a little more intense, but essentially to be explained away in the same swan's down terms.

How wrong they were. There had been nothing light about it and nothing easy. It had been no puppy-love, or calf-love or what have you, that he had felt. No vague, immature feeling of fondness for a graceful object that happened by a fluke of the dice to be of his own species and gender. Nothing of the kind. It had been love on the grand scale — personal, exclusive, discriminating; as precise, painful and stunning as a well-delivered uppercut to the jaw. No. Let the biographers and commentators skate as suavely as they liked over the episode and explain away as they would, in actual fact it had shaken him to the core. Pederasty might be agreeable to others (Sgricci, the impersonator, had seemed to do very well on it for one, and nobody had seemed much to mind, excepting the Venetian ladies, who'd thought it rather a waste of the man's talents), but it was not for him. He'd known this at the time — instinctively, deeply and utterly, as he'd always known it: however bland, however suavely looked on in enlightened circles, pederasty was not for him.

His body might claim to know otherwise. In fact, what with loss of appetite, and insomnia, and t'other thing (and everyone knew what that was, did they not?), at times it might even claim to know better. But from the very moment of Edleston's surrender, when instead of leaving the boy had knelt there on the floor pretending to tidy up the books, and then with a sob had scattered them to the four corners of the room again and sat down on his heels, and spread his hands, and looked at him with such yearning — from that very moment, he had known that pederasty was not for him. He couldn't go through with it. Not with Edleston; not with anyone who trusted him as Edleston did. Not with anyone who loved him as Edleston did. Not with anyone whom he himself loved, as he did Edleston.

It had taken minutes before he could trust himself to do anything in the way of approaching or touching the boy, but at length he had gained control over himself and had gone to sit beside Edleston on the floor, where he put his arms round him and drew him close, smothering the complicated feelings of desire and disgust that seemed inexplicably to be lodged inside him in exactly the same place and to exactly the same degree. Smothered them so well, in fact, that the resulting embrace might have been that of a parent animal to its cub. He had called him by his Christian name then, for the first time: John. 'John,' he'd said gently, 'Whatever you feel, whatever I feel; whatever you think you would like, and whatever I would like myself, the pledge we have exchanged is a pledge of friendship. Nothing less than friendship — a lifelong friendship as far as I am concerned, and the dearest and best I can ever hope to deserve — but nothing more, either. You understand?'

Edleston, however, perhaps more compromised, certainly less cowardly, would have none of this surrogate affection. 'No, I don't understand,' he'd whispered miserably, 'and no more do you. I understood you wanted me. The way you looked at me when I came in . . . The way you . . .' and his gaze travelled bewilderedly but with no flush of shame this time to the folds of the dressing-gown, a palm below waist-level, 'the way you moved. I still understand you want me.' Spurred by this piece of daring, he had then become more convinced and more vociferous. 'It wouldn't be wrong,' he said pleadingly, very loudly indeed. 'It wouldn't be all that wrong. How can it be wrong when two people care about each other as we do? Trust me just a moment. Wait, give me your hand . . .' and urgently he had taken possession of a hand, and holding it fast between his own had pushed aside the scarf he was wearing and begun to fumble with the neck of his shirt as if to loosen it. 'Please. Wait. Don't draw back now, I beg of you.' For a second, perhaps half a second, he had felt himself wavering. Then he had felt the warmth of Edleston's chest beneath his fingers. His hand recoiled of its own accord as if it had touched a hot plate, and he heard himself saying, in an angry tone which he had not in the least intended to use, 'Enough of that, Edleston. Get a hold of yourself for God's sake. We'll have the proctors on us if you go on squealing.' (Or words equally wounding. He might even have used the term 'stuck pig', since he was to be chided for this later on, but how could he have known at the time that Edleston was capable of doubly misunderstanding him?)

It had been a wretched moment altogether, followed by more wretched ones still. Hundreds of them. Thousands. For despite all his efforts, despite the obstinacy with which he had clung to the lean shoulders of his friend, shaking, cajoling, persuading, using all his eloquence to explain that he was not turning him down nor spurning him, but simply refusing to take advantage of him; despite a quick glance every now and again at the jewel hanging at Edleston's throat and a furtive little reminder to himself each time he did so, 'There goes half a coalmine, you nincompoop'; in brief, despite his resolve not to forfeit on any account both the friend and the jewel, this in the end was exactly what had happened.

The loss was not immediate. Somehow, amidst apologies and stammers from himself, and apologies and stammers from Edleston, and a hiccoughing crossfire of explanation discharged by both and heeded by neither, they had managed to worm their way out of the fix they landed themselves in on that ill-starred afternoon; and in the days that followed, gradually, tacitly, heads hanging a little low like soldiers who have shared dishonour and have no heart to criticize or blame a fellow combatant, they had drifted back into their former routine. Whenever a party on the river was organized Edleston had categorically refused to swim, but there was nothing very new in that: he never was a swimmer, never had been. When sitting together, even when sprawled informally on the grass, he had taken to choosing his position with the fastidiousness of a society hostess, and was always careful to dart off the moment the company began to dwindle; but that too was something he had done more or less from the very beginning. For the rest, they had resumed their rides (always in company now, though, and always with their horses well spaced), gone back to their drinking bouts and their reading sessions, had lounged about of an afternoon firing at empty wine bottles, bickering, joking, combing the dogs for fleas and generally conjugating the verb *s'ennuyer* in all its tenses, and — as far as outward appearances were concerned — had taken up the humdrum again from where they had interrupted it.

However, underneath the regularity and calm of the surface, there had run a current of unease which had affected them all — even Long, even the thick-skinned Bankes, even the couple of newer friends who had recently joined them. They were wilder for one thing, all of them. And — maybe in consequence — they were more unpopular. Scrapes of one kind or another became, not as before an enlivening exception, but the order of the day. When they weren't scrambling over walls in the small hours, fleeing from pursuers from other colleges and ripping their gowns to shreds in the process, they were rowing (not boat-rowing, but the other kind) with Trinity inmates — usually retaliating to provocation, but sometimes doing quite a bit of provoking on their own account. As far as he could remember, hardly a day had gone by without one or other of the group being confined to gates and walls. Which meant, naturally, that the others stayed inside as well to keep whoever it was company; which meant that they got bored again; which meant creating a little excitement to while away the time; which nearly always meant gates and walls again for someone else. And so it had gone on. His own gown became as tattered as a bottle-mop by the end of it; and the others' not much better. All of them developed gashed knuckles. Edleston, who was only involved in the day brawls and not even the worst of those but who none the less had a flair for fighting when seriously goaded, during one bout had dropped a paper-weight on his own foot instead of his opponent's, broken a toe, and had limped around for weeks. Long had split a lip and it had gone septic, making him look a proper bruiser. Their music too — on those few evenings that they were sober enough to make it — had been wilder. The restless undertow of the current had affected even that.

Indeed there had been one or two occasions when the current was so strong that it had sent bubbles to the surface where they could be seen by the others. Once, for example, in some classical context — perhaps it was the Symposium they had been discussing — the subject of pederasty had cropped up; and at this not only had Edleston done his usual trick of switching from green to pink like a chameleon on a rose-bush, but he himself had turned so silent of a sudden that Long, who happened to be sitting between them, had started and then looked from one to the other with a shrewd, quizzing look, much as to say, 'So that's the way the land lies, is it? Well, I'll be blowed!'

Another occasion had been more revealing still. Bankes had been carping on about Barnwell, and how plentiful the females were there, and how pliable: 'It's easy for you to be so superior, Byron,' he'd said crossly on being told to speak of something else for a change, 'you've crossed your darn Rubicon already. *Alea jacta est.* Or rather *ejacta est.* You ought to have pity on us lesser mortals. And you certainly ought to tell us more about how it went off. If we can't be actors, let us at least be part of the audience.' At which there'd been a general murmur of agreement. Legs were crossed, cushions lodged under backsides, and faces lifted in smiling anticipation. It had been impossible to disappoint them. His head turned away from Edleston, he had begun to relate.

He had been as brief and as vague as was possible under the circumstances: he had toned down, omitted, glossed over, and glisséed round. He had dwelt on the funny parts — the most uncomplimentary to himself — of which there were several. But they had plagued and insisted. 'What did the one you got in the end look like, Byron? Was she anything as pretty as Miss Curtis of the Hoope? What did she say while . . . you know what? What sort of an answer's that — you can't remember? Where did she take you? How did she *begin*, so to speak; how did she set *about* it? And then what did she do? And you? And then? And *then*?' . . . until he had just had to keep them happy and give them more or less the full chronicle.

When he had finished, while all the others were laughing and making comments, Edleston had fished out a handkerchief and made a distinct retching noise

104

into it. Even Bankes had raised his eyebrows over that one. Fortunately, this had taken place towards the end of term when the ordeal was nearing its close, and had been the last incident of its kind.

How had he managed to bear with it, he wondered now in afterthought? Those weeks of hypocrisy and masquerade, how had they ever passed? How had he been able to go on consorting with Edleston as he did (Edleston, who for all the upset between them was still the being he cared for most in the world); laughing with him, arguing with him, chatting with him of this and that and the other, and referring gaily to what they would do 'next term', when all the time he had made up his mind that all was finished between them and that there would be no 'next term' as far as their friendship was concerned? And how had he been able to stick by such a decision for so long, when nine-tenths of him had still cried out for Edleston and ten-tenths of Edleston had cried back?

The answer, of course, was simple, although he was not sure whether it would be believed: he had gone through with it because Edleston was a boy.

Because he was a *boy*, Lord Byron? he could hear posterity ask in surprise. Because homosexual love was frowned on in the society in which you moved? Because there was an outmoded law against it, which no judge in his right senses would ever have applied anyway? For a footling, *petit bourgeois* reason like that? You, a peer, the author-to-be of *Childe Harold* and *Don Juan*, who never cared a lump of sugar for public opinion? You who were shortly to flaunt it and tease it and snap your fingers at it as few had ever dared before? Surely you would not have us believe that this was the reason: that the dashing Lord Byron was on the run from a choirboy?

Yes, he could only reply: because Edleston was a boy; and because public opinion and his own coincided for once on the issue at stake. He was only eighteen at the time, remember. Not cowardly exactly, but unsure, and unhappy. That was why he had fled Cambridge a second time; why he had done everything in his power in the year that followed to avoid being sent back there; why he had resorted, time after time, to the ministrations of the celebrated French *entremetteuse* while in London, justly renowned for her expertise in guiding the wandering feet of many a young pilgrim like himself along the straight and open path to pleasure; why he had flirted his head off in Southwell with the local belles; and why, despite the zeal with which he had set about his various lessons in human topography, deep down inside he had all the while been miserable as a cur.

10   A Third Jog to the Memory

By now there was a faint but unmistakable air of
stalemate in the computer room. Motes of dust hung in
the air, flowers drooped over the rims of their vases.
The computer hummed along quietly, spewing out its
usual roll of unmarked paper with every appearance of
sulkiness. Now and again, breaking the *basso continuo*
of the machine, the stool gave a little squeak in response to the shiftings of its occupant.

The two assistants were stretched out symmetrically
on opposite ends of the sofa with coffee cups in their
hands, conferring with one another in lowered voices.
From her seat at the terminal behind them Anna could
hear snatches of their conversation: 'Time we went on
to the next stage,' they were saying. 'Language pretty
well tied up as it is.' 'High-powered historian arriving.'
'Want to be ready for the Los Angeles Congress.' 'Can't
waste any more time fiddling with inessentials.' She
cleared her throat to draw their attention to her
presence.

'Ah, Anna,' said the male assistant without turning
round, 'still at it? Fine. How's the old poofter coming
along? By the way,' he added, 'if you find you're
getting bogged down with whatever it is you're on to
now, just go on to something else. We're a bit pushed
for time. Hop about a bit. Try to cover a wider range of
subjects.'

'It was you who said stick to poetry and sex,' Anna reminded him, 'but, yes, of course, whatever you say. Only the thing is,' and she cleared her throat again, 'I've got a feeling I might be on the verge of discovering something really important at last. You see, I've just got the computer to admit quite openly that Byron was potty about Edleston and that that was the reason he stayed away from Cambridge as long as he did. Although,' she added, trying not to sound disappointed, 'it still won't quite admit that the Thyrza poems were written with Edleston in mind, or that they were in any way inspired by a homosexual love affair.'

'Where's the discovery then?' asked the man, using his cup to cover a yawn.

'I said *verge* of the discovery,' she corrected him. 'And I can't say for sure, but I know it's concealing something from me on the Thyrza front, because it's started to fall into contradiction about it.'

'Contradiction?' he said, snapping his mouth shut on the cup. 'Impossible! There's nothing contradictory about being fond of someone and not writing verses to them. Most of us do it all the time. You'd better face up to the fact that there's no connection between this Edleston of yours and Thyrza or Towser or whatnot, and go on to something else.'

'But there *must* be a connection of sorts,' Anna objected, gathering papers and books into a bundle and carrying them across to the sofa. 'Read some of the poems for yourself if you don't believe me: Thyrza of the poems sang beautifully; Edleston sang beautifully. Byron exchanged a pledge with Thyrza; he exchanged a pledge with Edleston. Thyrza died while Byron was on his first foreign tour, so did Edleston. I've compared dates and everything too. It all fits. There's no other explanation.'

'There ruddy well is, you bet,' the man said wearily, puffing out his cheeks. 'For one thing, Byron might easily have been carrying on with someone else at the same time as his affair with Edleston.' He smiled at his colleague on the far end of the sofa adding for the sake of provocation Anna thought, 'I wouldn't put it past him after what he got up to in Venice.'

'But this was *before* what he got up to in Venice,' she insisted. 'Before he was jaded and disillusioned; it was when he was young and trusting and sincere. Look at this on the print-out here; it's as clear as they come:

YOUR LETTER OF JULY 5TH 1807 STATES THAT YOU LOVED MR JOHN EDLESTON MORE THAN ANY HUMAN BEING. WAS THIS AN EXAGGERATION OR WERE YOU SINCERE?

A long pause follows,' she explained earnestly, looping the paper round her arm like an anchor rope and searching for the next printed reply, 'and then it says, quite simply and openly for a change:

I WAS SINCERE.

DO YOU AGREE THAT THE THYRZA CYCLE CONTAINS YOUR MOST IMPASSIONED AND INSPIRED LOVE LYRICS?

I DO.

AND WERE THEY THEREFORE WRITTEN TO THE PERSON YOU LOVED MORE THAN ANY HUMAN BEING?

THE WORDING OF YOUR QUESTION IS A TRIFLE LOOSE, ANNA, BUT THE ANSWER IS YES, THEY WERE.

THEREFORE THE THYRZA CYCLE WAS WRITTEN TO MR JOHN EDLESTON, WAS IT NOT?

Now you'd think it'd *have* to say yes at this point, wouldn't you?' she urged.

There was a moment's silence. 'You would,' said both assistants together, lowering their coffee-cups and showing sudden signs of interest.

'Well,' said Anna slowly, unable to prevent a trace of triumph entering into her voice, 'that's just what it doesn't. Instead it says: MY PATIENCE IS WEARING THIN. I SUGGEST YOU LOOK TO YOUR LOGIC. There's huffiness for you,' she added with a smile. 'It's not my logic that's at fault, it's its.'

'Impossible,' said the male assistant again, but less convincedly than before, 'impossible.' He squinted worriedly at the print-out. '*Wait* a minute, though,' he added, clicking his fingers castanet-fashion for a few moments and then rounding on his colleague with a frown. 'The parameters,' he told her, 'it's those darned, daft parameters of yours, that's what it is. I knew they'd give us nothing but trouble. The program can't confess to homosexuality because the anxiety parameters are still too high. So what does it do? It goes and buggers up its logic instead.' He brought a fist down on the table, slopping the coffee and scattering pollen and petals. 'There's only one thing for it: we'll just have to lower them again.'

'They're *not* all that low now, as a matter of fact,' the woman said, glancing calmly at the spilt coffee, 'because after we lowered them together, I put them up again.' She held up her hand to silence his protest and check the gill-like cheeks which were beginning to puff out sideways again, 'And I'm afraid we can't go lowering them a second time. You know my views on the matter: any further tinkering would be tantamount to messing about with the beliefs of a real brain.'

'You mean LB might go neurotic on us,' he scoffed.

'You know perfectly well what I mean,' she replied. 'I mean it might get into a muddle. We were agreed from the outset: each parameter can be shifted slightly either way for purposes of adjustment, and can be shifted back into its original position, but none can be shuffled about indefinitely without repercussion on the system. So far the deep memory is probably unaffected by the

110

changes we've made, but the program will already have had to erase some incompatible beliefs from its intermediary set, and we can't very well ask it to re-introduce them without any side effects whatever, can we now? At the very least it'll want to know why it has changed its mind.'

The man shrugged. 'Well, we must do *something*,' he said, picking up his coffee-cup again and downing the contents in a gulp, 'and quickly. We've got this famous history don arriving tomorrow. We can't serve him up a program that contradicts itself. Unless he's a Hegelian, of course, which I don't think he is. Of course if I had *my* say in the matter I'd be inclined to scrap the parameters altogether and leave it at that.'

His colleague gazed at him stonily. 'No.'

'No,' Anna was quick to second her. 'No, you can't do a thing like that to Albè; it'd be worse than a lobotomy. Couldn't we do something else? I don't know . . . alter one of the other parameters instead — to compensate, as it were?'

The couple on the sofa looked at her in surprise and then at one another.

'She has a point there.'

'Yes, she has a point there. At a pinch — at a *pinch*, mind you — I suppose we could do that: try and counteract the increased anxiety on the homo side by stepping up the interest values on the hetero one.'

'Which might be the very thing that's needed for the language too,' Anna went on hurriedly. 'I know my job is counted as more or less finished, but the language still isn't *quite* right, not even after the last adjustment we made. For one thing, it's a bit on the pedantic side sometimes — not flippant enough, if you see what I mean . . .' ('A flippant computer being another of the things we try to avoid,' remarked the female assistant

111

aside to her colleague, who mouthed a groan in reply.) '. . . and for another it's suddenly gone a bit prudish about certain topics. One thing I noticed, for instance: it simply can't bear talking about prostitutes or brothels or anything like that now – not even when I give it the Professor's code number instead of my own; and yet those are subjects it's never objected to before. And rightly, seeing that Byron himself discussed them quite freely with other men.'

'Ah well, that clinches it then in my view,' said the woman assistant getting briskly to her feet. 'Two birds with one stone. We'll go ahead and up the hetero interest and see if we can't right things that way. It won't be as easy as it sounds, of course, because the program hasn't got a global frame on heterosexuality as far as I remember; so it'll mean touching up all the various items in the vocabulary that have a bearing on the subject – things like . . .' She paused for a moment, evidently trying to decide what these items could be.

'Like breasts and genitals,' prompted her colleague from the other end of the sofa. 'That's all: breasts and genitals. Nothing complex about heterosexuality from a man's point of view. Easy as pie,' and he flexed his rubber soles complacently.

'If that's what you think, then your mind is a good deal cruder than the machine's,' the woman snapped at him, crossing over to the terminal and beginning to loosen her fingers in a professional way. Anna noted, however, that whatever the alterations were they were performed very quickly. She knew it was foolish, but she could not help wondering whether, apart from the language, they would make any difference to Albè's attitude towards herself.

'I'd go easy on the genitals,' came a warning voice from the sofa where the male assistant was still sitting.

'Just raise the index a fraction and no more. Think of the League of Byron Lovers and how much they're coughing up. We don't want to shock the wits out of them.' Then came more squeaking of soles and a prolonged chuckle. 'Although . . . no,' he amended, 'on second thoughts, if the choice is to be between a straitlaced Byron and a scurrilous one, they'll probably prefer the latter. So go ahead. Lay it on thick. If err we must, then we'd better err on the right side.'

The woman gave a final tap to the keys. 'There is no need to err at all,' she replied. 'The balance may be delicate, but I think it's established now.' She turned to Anna, who had been listening interestedly to the exchange, 'Now you can go back to your checking,' she told her, in the condescending voice to which Anna had by now become accustomed. 'For this afternoon anyway. Only my colleague is right: in the time that remains, go on to something different for a change. With all this Cambridge stuff, and Thyrza and whatnot, you do seem to have got yourself into a bit of a rut.'

'OK, if you say so,' Anna agreed. 'Only I'll have to ask it *one* more question about brothels and so on, won't I? Otherwise I'll have nothing to check against.'

The male assistant chuckled again from the sofa, smirking as wide as the gills would allow. 'Then ask it about Byron's performance with the ladies there,' he suggested. 'That might even settle the pansy question for you, too.'

'Very well,' she replied, taking the suggestion quite seriously. 'Good idea. That's exactly what I'll do.'

113

11 Memoirs (Mostly) Proper

. . . Shabby. As he had tried to make Edleston understand when giving his spoken account of the matter,
the performance had been shabby. The lady in charge
of operations might well raise her hands in mock
stupor as she totted up the number of gratifications for
which he was to pay, and exclaim that never, no never
before had she seen such a young gentleman putting
up such a brave showing at this first attempt: why, that
made three separate 'straights', one 'special', which
came out just a little more expensive, and one 'flier',
which she would throw in with the rest as a bonus; her
employees might well gasp with admiration — every
whit as spurious — as he drilled his way through their
obliging ranks, lifting petticoat after petticoat and leaving the imprint of his attention beneath each; the
friend who had accompanied him might equally well
squeeze his arm as they went out into the street again
and hiss, 'Byron, what the deuce?' and clap him on the
back, and throw back his head and let out a great
whistle of glee; he himself knew it had been a failure.
Not a technical failure, exactly. No, not that. If he had
needed any proof of his manhood — which he supposed he had, or he wouldn't have gone to one of those
establishments in the first place, let alone gone back, as
he subsequently had, time after time — then proof he
had certainly obtained: he liked woman, all right; he

liked *women*. He liked them and he more than liked them. He liked the smell of them, and the touch of them, and most telling of all he liked the mysterious entrance to them, an entrance which seemed, like a seaweed-lined cleft in a rock, to lead to a whole smugglers' hoard of treasure inside. So that was not where the trouble lay. His failure had been of a different kind: a sentimental failure, if you like; a failure, not of the body, nor even of the mind, which had gone along very happily with the rest of him and seethed its way to much the same explosion of release, but of the heart. Quite simply, his heart had not been in his play. And where had it been instead? Why, with Edleston in Cambridge.

So he had proved nothing. Nothing; except that every time a woman's face lay beneath him (and the second face at least had been young and pretty, and either very good at acting or else genuinely pleased with what it was about), what he regularly found himself wishing was that it were the white, serious face of his choirboy friend — or, *force majeure*, the nape of his neck — that he was looking at; and that when he buried his head amongst ribbons and lace and inhaled the heady smell of powder and musk and soft, warm skin, and his body went about its business with no more ado, what he yearned for instead was to nose his way into a plain linen shirt and place his lips on the smooth, flat chest beneath that smelt of soap, and occasionally of horses, and that wore as its only ornament the stone he himself had provided. Not the lifting of petticoats, but the lowering of breeches — at any rate those particular breeches; that was what his heart was set on. Now, as before, and more than before.

So he had failed with the professional exorcists, but that was hardly surprising. How then had he fared

115

amongst the amateurs? Well, after a year spent flirting with any and every possible female that had come his way, after the more subtle but none the less teasing excitement of pressing hands, returning dropped fans and cast-off ribbons, writing verses up to the very limit of the permissible and a little beyond, of breathing down *décolletés*, and of using, according to the rules, nothing more heated than the eyes for the warming up of the quarry, here too he had to admit to failure. Here too, try as he might to oust it, the shadow of Edleston was still present, interposed like a screen between him and . . . And what? Fulfilment? Heigh ho! There was none of *that* to be had in Harrogate or Southwell. Achievement? Precious little of that either, although more than the outsider would suspect. Involvement, then? Yes, that was it: the shadow of Edleston had come between him and involvement. He could flirt as outrageously as he liked, and breathe heavily, and sigh and glare; place his fingers on the stem of each delicate flower; squeeze tighter and tighter until picking point was all but reached (and there were a lot more tedious ways of passing the time between the sexes, he had since discovered). But somehow, each time he was on the verge of losing himself in the eyes of whichever Miss it happened to be, he would find himself thinking of the dark, fringed eyes of Edleston, and: boomp! like a faulty bassoon his heart would skip a beat, and he would make his excuses to the lady and draw defeatedly aside. (Although, strange to say, this unmanly behaviour of his, together with the limp — the two things of which he was most bitterly ashamed — far from disgracing him, had done wonders for his reputation among members of the fairer sex; and by the time the year was out they were after him like a pack of harriers.)

116

It was therefore in an abject frame of mind that he finally gave in to his mother's pleas and everyone else's unasked advice, and returned to Cambridge a second time, to face his destiny there. He knew that it was unconditional surrender this time: he was more deeply in love with Edleston than ever before, wretched at having spent a whole year away from him to no avail whatever; lonely too by now; and although no longer frightened, still worried by this hungering urge inside him, and still unable to countenance it fully. Added to which, now that he had made up his mind to give in to the urge, he was also not a little jealous. For judging from the few, non-committal letters which he had received from Edleston, Cambridge life seemed to have been going on apace during his absence, and Edleston himself to have taken up with a number of new fast-living friends whom he didn't like the sound of at all. Indeed the only positive aspect of his return — apart from the joy of being reunited with Edleston — was that in his dudgeon he had dieted fiercely over the past months, taken a lot of exercise, and lost an amazing amount of weight. He was returning, therefore, not the plump, pasty-faced individual who had abashedly used to hold his breath when aware that the sylphlike Edleston was watching him, but a slim, fit, muscular and faintly suntanned one — unattainable idol of the Southwell belles, favoured client of Mme X's tried establishment, and (perhaps) even a future poet of some renown, seeing that he had a volume of scribblings in his pocket which had already been accepted for publication.

Yet none of these minor accomplishments, he realized — not even the slimming — counted for much when measured against the unknown length and depth of the step that he was about to take. He was going

117

back. His heart in his hand, or on his sleeve, or in some other miserably exposed position, he was going back to the battlefield from which he had fled; back to the rack; back to recover that branch of himself which he had hacked off and stuffed into a dark cupboard, only to find it a year later blossoming away in the darkness the size and strength of a tree.

This time, however (and no matter how many times he had used the phrase before, *this* time he really meant it), there would be no more struggle and no more mutilation. His mind was made up: he would let the rack pull him the way it listed. If it listed to perversion then to perversion he would go. And proudly — as long as Edleston went with him. What with all the poets and playwrights and painters and philosophers who had gone that way already, they would at least be in good company.

In the event, though, resolutions, scruples, racks and battlefields his benighted ar—e! For when at last he had gained composure enough to leave his rooms and to venture a stroll down Trinity walks (always the best place to engineer a chance meeting in Cambridge, not to mention by far the most romantic, thanks to the limes and the chestnut trees and what have you), he and Edleston had crossed paths without so much as recognizing each other. So there was your eternal passion for you!

Well, no, come, it had not gone quite so badly as that: he had recognized Edleston all right, although it had taken him a few moments to do so, but Edleston had not recognized *him* at all, and had merely blinked, nodded politely as to a stranger he had mistaken for an acquaintance, and gone on his way. (Which in the happiest of hypotheses, he reasoned, proved that this new thinness and brownness he had acquired in Southwell had altered his appearance indeed, and greatly to the better; but in the saddest, of course, proved things that he couldn't even bear to contemplate.)

So now, after a second day of waiting and nail-nibbling, and of promenading foolishly up and down the walks in the vain hope of bumping into Edleston again, he'd had to send a note to his short-sighted and short-memoried innamorato to inform him that Lord Byron was returned to University and would be pleased if Mr Edleston would deign to come round and call on him. Again: so much for your eternal passion.

Here he was then, back in exactly the same position of one year ago, waiting in a fidget in his rooms for Edleston's knock. The only variants being: first, that not only his person but his rooms too looked a little different now (having been occupied during his absence by one Skinner Matthews, reputedly a clever fellow, and fortunately of clean habits by the looks of things); second, that he had a new servant with him (the Boyce of dishonest memory, to Mrs B's delight had finally had to go); and third, that this time the Reverend George was lying gagged and blindfolded in a chest somewhere in the depths of the sea or on the bed of the River Cam. Silenced for good. Dead, he hoped. *This* time, with the Reverend safely out of the picture, there was to be no wavering, no drawing back: Edleston could have him on his own terms — mind, body, soul; as much of him as he wished, for as long as he wished.

Providing, of course, that Edleston wished. But did he? That was the question. Chewing on his last standing nail he began to rehearse a few openings which he thought might serve to ease them both over the inevitable awkwardness of their meeting and at the same time give him an insight into Edleston's intentions. Speed to the door as soon as the knock came, throw it open. 'Edleston! You have been in my mind for an average of ten hours a day for this past year!' No, that would never do. Sit sultry-faced in a chair and wait for Edleston to speak. No. Smile wordlessly and open wide his arms. Possibly. But no. Affect politeness — distance; speak of goings on in Southwell and London. Affect ease; speak as if they had left one another an hour before, 'What time's choir practice this evening, Edleston? Have a slice of brawn.' No, no, and no. None of them pleased him; he must just wait, and sweat it out, and be himself.

When the knock came, however, his mind went conveniently blank and he walked straight to the door and opened it without fuss. His heart soared, hovered, and them tumbled to earth again: it was Hobhouse, a friend of Matthews; they knew each other slightly from the preceding year and disliked each other slightly more.

'May I come in?' the visitor asked stiffly. 'I'm sorry to barge in on you like this but Matthews has left some books here and asked me to pick them up for him.'

(Well don't stand there fiddling, go ahead. And be quick about it for God's sake.) 'Ah. Do, please,' he managed to say civilly when he had settled his heart in its rightful place again. 'I'm afraid I hoofed poor Matthews out of his chambers in something of a hurry. As a matter of fact he might do better to leave some of his belongings here. I may be off again shortly, you see. I don't know. I haven't yet made up my mind.'

Hobhouse's stubby and rather commonplace features melted into a smile, making him look younger and nicer. He seemed to have forgotten their earlier dislike of one another, or else to have revised it in the interval. 'Ah, yes. We know something of your volatility from your tutor,' he said with a chuckle. 'He never stopped telling us: "Don't touch that, don't move this, leave that table be; I warn you, Lord Byron is a man of *tumultuous* passions." Matthews was enchanted by the "tumultuous" — he can't wait to get to know you.'

So Skinner Matthews wanted to make his acquaintance, did he? Was he too lurking on the stairway? He peered anxiously over the square outline of Hobhouse's head and shoulders, but noted with relief that the caller was presently unaccompanied. ' "Tumultuous" may prove a tiring reputation to live up to,' he replied automatically, 'but please tell Matthews from me that I too, on my part, should be delighted to meet him. I've heard he is vastly amusing. Tell him that as well while you're about it. I don't see why I should be the only one to be kept on my mettle.'

His visitor smiled again more widely, and closing the door behind him stepped fully into the room and began to converse in a leisurely fashion about university matters, rocking benevolently from the balls of his feet to his heels (the danger-signal, he feared, of one about to subside into a chair with an afternoon at his disposal).

'The books, Hobhouse!' he brought him up smartly. 'I mustn't be wasting your time. You came for some books. I hope they haven't become jumbled up with mine by mistake,' and quickly he began to examine the packages and cases that were stacked against the wall waiting the attention of the formidable young Fletcher, his new valet.

'Oh, never mind the books,' said Hobhouse good-naturedly, bending at the knee and feeling around behind him for a seat. 'I see you've changed things

121

already. When Matthews was in residence he used to keep a chair just about here.'

'A chair? Forgive me. Do please sit down.' The words eked out of him ungraciously.

'I'm not intruding on your time, by any chance?'

'Not a bit. Not a bit.'

'Ah,' said the Hobhouse creature happily, lowering himself on to the chaise-longue and propping his feet on the fender. 'Now, tell me. I hear you've turned into something of a poet while you've been away. It's a treat for me to meet a poet. I do quite a bit of writing myself.'

Splendid, he told himself wryly. Just what was wanted. A large, irremovable lump of literary ambition wedging itself between him and Edleston at this, the moment of their long-awaited reunion. 'Splendid,' he said wanly, giving a quick glance out of the window to see if he could spot Edleston. 'Do tell me, what have you put your hand to so far?'

'Well,' said Hobhouse, confirming his worst fears by rolling sideways and digging energetically into his pocket, 'I was hoping you'd ask me that, because as luck would have it, I have a little something with me that I jotted down a couple of days ago with the Whig Club in mind . . .'

It was only five minutes of the clock, but something like five hundred lines of solid, classical-pillared prose later, when Edleston finally arrived. Hobhouse, who in the short space of his sitting there seemed already to have acquired something of the proprietorial, faintly jealous air which was to characterize his side of their friendship for life, left off his reading, gathered his papers together with all the hall-marks of huff and crammed them back into his pocket, badly folded. 'I didn't realize you were expecting another visit, Byron,' he mumbled. 'Please excuse me. Most inopportune of

122

me. You've only just got back. You have friends to see. Of course. Of course. *Ubi major, minor cessat.* Edleston, is it not?' he added, half rising and stretching out a hand, 'The famous — what's it? — soprano?'

'Alto,' Edleston corrected him. (So the voice at least had not changed.)

'Alto. I see. High anyway. Then what'll it turn into? Basso?'

Edleston flushed (another welcome sign of his not having altered much in the year's interval) and shrugged his shoulders, 'I don't think so, somehow,' he said with an abashed smile. 'Tenor more likely.'

'Ah,' said Hobhouse on a friendlier note, appeased no doubt by the boy's embarrassment, 'that'll come with the beard, I suppose; a double surprise for you.'

Edleston nodded. 'Yes,' he said quietly, staring in apparent absorption at the patterns of the carpet, 'when it comes it'll be a surprise all right.'

There was a moment's uneasy silence as Hobhouse made an appraising examination of Edleston's jawline. Stealthily, following Hobhouse's glance he took a look at it himself. No moustaches, he noted relievedly, no reddened skin or scratches left by a novice-drawn razor, no coarsening of the features, or thickening of the neck: to all outward appearance Edleston was still every inch the ethereal, ivory-sculptured fledgling that he remembered. Perhaps (and he gauged a trifle enviously the level of the boy's shoulders with respect to his own) there were now a few more inches to be accounted for, but that was all.

The inner changes, on the other hand, were not so easy to assess — especially not with the amiable Hobhouse planted there between them — and these were the ones that worried him more deeply. Edleston hadn't even looked him in the face yet or said hello, let

123

alone smiled or tried to convey a message. Was he still wearing the pledge he wondered, stealing another glance at Edleston's neck? And did it mean anything if he was? Now if only this well-meaning intruder of a Hobhouse would take himself off with the speed and unexpectedness with which he had arrived, he would be able to discover both these things for himself and put an end to his misery. For once alone with him, he could take Edleston's chin in the palm of his hand, force the head upwards (even if it meant standing on tiptoe to do so), examine the neck for the pendant, prise the lids open if necessary with the tips of his fingers, and stare Edleston straight in the eye and read his fate there. After all, the possibilities as to what he would find were only two: love or indifference, union or banishment. Under the present circumstances, however, whatever message Edleston might have in store for him had to be interpreted on its journey to or from the carpet, dressed with the formality that a third party's presence imposed.

'Delighted to see you back, Byron.'

'Delighted to see you, Edleston.'

'You've changed. I didn't recognize you the other day. At least, for a *moment* I thought it was you; and then I thought it couldn't be.'

'I recognized you, though.'

'But *I* haven't changed.'

'Haven't you? Haven't you? Not at *all*?'

Silence for a moment. Then dismissively, 'Hardly at all. What's happened to your hair, by the way? It's gone quite a different colour.'

'Oh, bleached from all the sweating I've done, I suppose. I've been taking a lot of exercise lately.'

'So I can see.'

'Good. Because it cost me a great deal of effort. Staved

124

in a rib, too, while I was about it.'

Edleston, after a fugitive glance at the ribcage, 'I'd begun to think you'd abandoned the university for good.'

'Well, no. I may have thought so myself at one time, but if so I've changed my mind. As you can see.' . . . Go on now — infuse the words with a little daring, for goodness' sake . . . 'I've changed my mind about quite a number of things.' . . . Bolder, be bolder . . . 'About um . . . one thing in particular, if you follow me: a subject we used to disagree on in the past.'

'Ha! The tumultuous passions again.' This was Hobhouse, making them both start.

Edleston remained impassive and continued politely to address the carpet, 'And Boatswain — is he back too?'

'He's lodged with a friend in Nottinghamshire for the time being. I'm told there are regulations against keeping dogs in your rooms this year.'

'Oh those. No one pays much attention to them. And it's only gun-dogs that are forbidden anyway. I think you could get away with Boatswain: he looks more like a bear than a dog.'

'You mean there are no regulations against bears? Well, in that case, if they won't let me have Boatswain I'll have a bear instead.'

Edleston, with a sudden burst of naturalness, 'Oh, I wish you would. I love bears.'

'But only if I decide to stay, that is.'

'And you haven't decided?'

'I can't. Not until I've been here for a while and got the feel of the place. I need to see my friends first.'

Edleston, stilted again, to the pile of the carpet, 'Does your staying depend on them then?'

'On some of them more than others.'

'Ah, I see.'

Silence.

'Well, don't go leaving until you've seen Matthews,' Hobhouse again. 'I know you'll hit it off famously the pair of you.'

The opportunity was slight, but not to be missed. 'Then why not go and fetch the fellow straight away?' he put in quickly, smiling at Edleston and then turning to Hobhouse with a show of enthusiasm. 'I know what: I'll get Fletcher to lay on a cold supper for us later, and we can make an evening of it. Edleston and I', he added, gesturing nonchalantly towards Edleston but taking good care not to touch him, 'will wait for you here. How's that?'

'Why not? The sooner the better. Capital idea!'

Hobhouse leapt obligingly from the chaise-longue, only to clap a hand to his forehead and sink down on the cushions again. 'No good. Have to wait,' he explained as he sank. 'Matthews won't be back yet. I remember now: he's gone off swimming for the afternoon. Hired himself a boat to dive from.' He settled himself deeper into the upholstery and made a face, 'Mud; gnats, weeds in your gizzard!' he said laughing. 'But there; I suppose *de gustibus non disputandum est*, ha ha!'

'Ha, ha,' echoed Edleston faintly.

'Ha, ha,' he echoed himself.

And so it was that the reunion with Edleston — the *true* one, for you could hardly count as a reunion this stiff little *ouverture à trois* which preceded it — took place in the water. An aquatic reunion. *Rapprochement dans l'eau*. Although, to be exact, it took place two feet *under* the water, and not with Edleston at all, but with someone rather different.

It was his own doing, of course. It was he who

suggested they go down to the river to look for Matthews (anything to get Hobhouse out of the room, he told
himself, close to panic, as he watched the bulky torso
ensconce itself among the cushions with a final twitch
of permanence); he who whisked his tardy visitor
cheerfully through the doorway and down the spiral
stairs, dragging a surprised and reluctant Edleston in
their wake; he who tracked down Hobhouse's friend,
Skinner Matthews (not diving, as it turned out, nor
even swimming, but reclining under the shade of a
canopy on a boat moored some way down the river,
fully dressed, and holding forth to a group of admiring
listeners for anything as if he were a pampered Roman
orator); and he who stripped off first and, deaf to all
protestations, persuaded Edleston to plunge alongside
him into the water.

'Quick. I beg of you,' he urged in a whisper while
Hobhouse's back was momentarily turned away from
them both, braced in a titanic struggle of pulling off
boots and stockings and rolling up breeches. 'Let's get
away from the fellow. Let's get away from the lot of 'em
while we have the chance. You can swim, can't you, if
you want to?' he inquired in afterthought.

Edleston nodded silently, his mouth hanging open
like one winded.

'Then follow me,' he hissed, grabbing hold of the
boy's shirt which in their haste had not been doffed,
and sliding into the water. 'I know of a place where we
can be alone and talk. I beseech you, Edleston,' (giving
the shirt a great tug), 'follow me, quick; I must talk to
you or burst.'

They swam in silence. At first, for Hobhouse's benefit, they struck out towards the moored boat, but
then leaving it to their right by a good ten yards or so
they made instead for a bridge upstream, passed under

it, and swam on until they reached a large, trailing willow on the far bank.

With a signal to Edleston, who was lagging behind by now puffing slightly, he ducked under the foliage and emerged in the sequestered pool that he knew to lie behind, and clambering out on to the bank turned to watch his beloved's arrival. His heart was hammering against his ribs as if he had swum the Hellespont (a feat he would like to accomplish some day, as a matter of fact, given the chance), but he knew the hammering had nothing to do with the swimming.

A moment or two later Edleston pushed his way through the leaves like an otter — his hair, darkened by the water, swept back evenly from the forehead and drops of moisture glistening on the brows and lashes. To an expert eye like his own such total wetness should of course have indicated that the fellow hadn't been holding his head far enough out of the water and was therefore either a better swimmer than he made out or else a very poor one indeed, but he could only think of the beauty it added to the face and head. Such beauty. It shone out like a mute challenge to the rest of the universe — 'Sky, you are dull,' it seemed to be saying, 'trees, you are graceless; swans you are flumpity, for here in all my splended wetness am I.' It was almost painful to watch. Especially to one in his own position who still didn't know what was going on inside the head or behind the face and so desperately needed to find out.

He swallowed, and bit the inside of his cheek until he tasted blood, and went on watching.

'Hey! I think it's safe to leave the water now,' he called out softly when he saw that the otter had come to a halt in the middle of the pool and was making no move to approach any nearer. He patted the bank invitingly. 'Later we may have to go back and join the others, but here we can sit for a while in peace and quiet and talk without being interrupted.'

An invitation, however, which curiously enough Edleston, digging in his toes suddenly after his run of unquestioning docility, declined.

'Not coming out,' he panted, spitting a piece of weed from between his teeth and treading water resolutely, 'staying here.'

And he evidently meant what he said. The next part of the conversation, in fact — intense, intimate and lengthy though it was — had to be carried out with himself sitting perched on the bank (lame foot hidden among the rushes on account of its nakedness), and with Edleston's beautiful but disembodied head bobbing about in the water in front of him. (For Edleston, too, as it turned out, had something to hide.)

'I am back.'

'So I see.'

'I am back because of you.'

'That I don't see so clearly.'

'Because the struggle is over and I have no fight left in me. I have come back to give in to you. On your terms.'

'Ah,' said Edleston, spitting his words, but only on account of more duckweed. 'It took you long enough to make up your mind.'

'It was a hard fight. If you no longer want me, I will go away again.'

'No, don't do that. Stay.'

'You mean that as an answer?'

'I mean it as an answer.'

A flat exchange, he supposed looking back on it, for a moment of high romantic drama. Not the sort of thing that would have carried much weight on the stage: two lovers charged to bursting point; misunderstandings, partings, a year's estrangement; and then merely, 'Don't do that. Stay.' 'You mean it as an answer?' 'I mean it as an answer.' And yet to himself at the time so profoundly moving and satisfying that all he could do was to let out a groan and fling himself backwards on the grass, the simple word 'stay' resounding in his ears like the sweetest note of music he had ever heard.

He lay there, gazing at the shafts of late afternoon sunlight as they pierced the willow leaves, his body wet and relaxed, his mind, for the first time in . . . could it be two years already since that evening in the Chapel when he and Edleston had first become aware of one another . . . ? Yes, with his mind achieving something like peace for the first time in nearly two years; and, haltingly at first, but with growing speed and eloquence as he got under way, he began to speak to Edleston without reserve, from the depths of his heart. He spoke of his love for him, of the torments he had gone through on account of it, of the pangs of indecision he had suffered, and of the terrible wrestling match he had sustained with the Reverend George from which he had finally emerged victorious. 'Can you ever forgive me', he asked tremulously, not daring to wait for an answer, 'when it is my cowardice, and that alone, which has kept us apart so foolishly and so long?'

Due either to the wetness of his person, or to that of the setting, or perhaps as an unconscious tribute to Edleston, who still could be heard floundering about in the pool below interjecting the odd splutter of comment now and again, the metaphors that came to him for his confession were chiefly watery ones. 'The tide was sweeping me forward,' he expounded lyrically to the branches above, 'I could no longer struggle against its

130

current. The loss of you parched me. I have thirsted for you all this time.' ('Me too, me too,' interjected Edleston at this point, despite his lack of breath apparently persisting in his acrobatics in the river.) 'The sluices are lifted now. My love for you has the force, the sweep of a cascade. I cannot stem it; cannot dam it. It must carry me forward where it will. Wherever it leads us, whatever we may find, calm or storm we will brave it together. With you by my side, Edleston, I have no fear of drowning.'

And so on in this vein. When the watery metaphors had dried themselves up, light-headed – giddy almost – with the relief of having unburdened himself, he closed his eyes. Would the happiness that lay ahead be equal to that of the present moment, he wondered? Would any happiness, ever? He doubted it: no one in the world at any future time could be as happy as he now felt; no one in the past could ever have been so happy. And hugging the moment to him greedily, he savoured it to the full, willing time to stop.

After another moment or so's reverie, however, receiving no response from his listener other than gurgles, he opened his eyes again and sat up; to discover with a shock of dismay that all that was left of the beautiful, water-glossed features of his beloved Edleston was a crescent of bubbles on the surface of the pool. He leapt to his feet, horrorstruck. What was that that he'd been blathering on about? No fear of drowning? By the Gods, how could he have been such a nincompoop? Edleston *was* drowning! Here he'd been, sitting day-dreaming on the bank, while within oar's distance of him the being he held dearest in the world was drowning before his very eyes!

With a cry he flung himself forward, hitting the surface of the water with the flat of his belly, and began

131

to grope wildly with arms and legs over the spot at which he had seen the bubbles. Emptiness. Panic seized him; he tried to grope deeper, flapping like a duck on the surface until he remembered that if he were to go under properly he must first expel the air from his lungs. This he did immediately. 'Fizz' went his breath; 'glop' went the wavelets in his ears. And then in sudden silence he sank slowly beneath the green, cloudy water and was able to look about him.

The first thing he saw was a patch of whiteness to his left. He made a grab at it, and then another, and with a sob of relief that caused him to open his mouth wide and let the water in, felt material of some kind beneath his hand: Edleston's shirt, and flesh beneath the material — Edleston himself.

Coughing and spluttering, and thanking his stars that all the boxing and wrestling he had done over the past months had made him so robust in the top half that he was able to carry his burden with little difficulty, he dragged Edleston's limp body to the bank and heaved it up on to the grass above. Hardly aware of what he was doing, let alone stopping to ask himself whether it was the right thing to do in the circumstances or not, he laid the boy face downwards and began thumping him hard on the back to get the water out of him. How long had the poor creature been under, he wondered? A minute? Two minutes? Three? He yanked the head round unceremoniously and put his lips feverishly to Edleston's nostrils to see if he could feel air coming out of them. Could you drown in three minutes, he wondered? Surely not. Oh, surely, surely not.

Fortunately, the answer to this seemed to be no, that you couldn't; since at the fifth or so thump Edleston moaned, then belched loudly, and after a couple more whacks began to breathe again, grampus fashion; still in a faint, but recognizably on the mend. (And even like *that*, he couldn't help remarking — belching and blowing though it was — the face was still beautiful enough to take your breath away.)

Predictably enough, now that the danger was past and there was no call for him to do so, he felt himself beginning to shake with fright, and stretching his own body alongside that of Edleston's he put his arms round the long, wet form and held it tight. The posture, he realized, was not one that would give rise to very favourable comment if anyone were to come upon them: he naked to the waist, shuddering rhythmically; Edleston, head thrown back, abandoned in his arms. But as luck would have it the tree screened them pretty closely from the river, and there weren't that many people about. And anyway who gave a d——n if they saw or not. He had already been deprived of Edleston for a year by his own pettifogging notions of decency — by trying to live up to an idealized portrait of himself which bore no likeness to his real character; after a year's absence he had been tantalizingly re-united to him for a moment in the presence of a stranger; and now, alone with him at last after all the hindrances in a setting of romantic seclusion, he had nearly been deprived of him for good and all by a tendency to relish the sound of his own voice. So who *cared* if people saw them, if tongues wagged, if the prudes frowned and the enlightened tittered mockingly behind their handker- chiefs: he had got Edleston safe in his arms at long last, and he would never let go of him again.

Never. Henceforth they would be inseparable. They would set up house together like — what were the ladies' names? Miss Ponsonby and Lady Eleanor Butler. His other friends might be surprised at such a step —

133

they too were in possession of rather a different portrait; Fletcher might raise his eyebrows when he called them in the morning with their glasses of hock and seltzer; Hanson might hiccough over the joint accounts, Mrs B. might choke on 'em; but who *cared*? Who gave a tea-leaf or a fish's udder? He had quashed the Reverend George — far and away the stoniest obstacle in his path — and he would quash the rest.

Edleston's breathing was back to normal now. Tenderly he rolled the body over. Silly ass of a choirboy, he thought fondly to himself; why the deuce hadn't he admitted he was tired? Why had he insisted on staying in the water like that all this time? He pushed back a lock of Edleston's hair, letting it curl limply round his finger for a moment, and traced a path round the curve of the neck into the hollow of the throat. Slowly he undid two studs of the shirt — partly to aid Edleston's breathing and partly to spy inside for a second and make sure he was still wearing the jewel he had given him.

He was. Good. He did the studs up again and smiled; it amused him to see that the ducking had made the shirt quite transparent, and that the stone, pink and glistening, shone through the material in such a curious way as to make it seem the tip of a woman's . . .

God Almighty! No longer smiling, he drew in his breath with a whistle. For there beneath the thin veil of linen which stuck to the skin like a skin itself, slightly below the pink protuberance of the jewel, as symmetrical to it as the points of an isosceles or what-you-may-call-it triangle, were two other protuberances: Edleston's chest was not as flat as he had imagined it to be. More rubies? Brooches? Medallions? No. Breasts. Believe it or not, Edleston grew breasts!

Not very full ones mind you, he decided on closer

inspection; not much of a setting for the rubies; cups rather than cupolas; but very definitely breasts: two springy little hillocks — firm, fleshy, pretty as shells.

He held his breath and stretching out a forefinger brushed it cautiously over the tip of the breast: it concentrated to a point, as if drawing itself to attention — a breast in full working order. Well flay me and sunburn me, he thought to himself in stupefaction! No wonder Edleston sang like a cherub, blushed like a peach and retained a marble-smooth jawline. No wonder he refused to swim in company and kept his shirt on when he did. Edleston was a hermaphrodite.

Wait a minute, though. Wait a *minute*: was he even that? And still more cautiously he drew the exploring hand downwards, piqued rather than otherwise by his discovery. All these months of heart-searching he thought crossly as he groped, and of fighting against his conscience, trying to get used to the idea that he was irredeemably in love with a boy, and now it seemed that the struggle had been unnecessary. His hand delved deeper into the secret recesses of Edleston's lower belly and thighs. Yes, totally unnecessary. For as far as he could make out through the layers of cloth that separated his index finger from what lay underneath, Edleston was not a hermaphrodite, nor even a eunuch: Edleston was a woman.

His pique subsiding, he allowed his hand to probe further, undoing buttons, uncovering, opening, penetrating. No doubt about it, he decided: female; Edleston was a she; not a Mr Edleston, but a Miss Edleston.

Well, well, well. He withdrew his hand and did the buttons up again — quickly and summarily, since the Miss Edleston's eyelashes had begun to flutter fast — and lay down again, thinking very hard. In place of the pique (natural enough when a lover has deceived you

135

on such an important matter as gender), and the curiosity (natural enough too), what he now felt was something more like disappointment. *Not* so natural. He pulled himself up on his elbow, and absent-mindedly wiping his forefinger on the grass, did up a few more of the buttons he had left undone and took stock of the creature that had, or so he couldn't help thinking, cheated him of his choirboy love. There it lay, a stranger; five foot ten inches of rebellious femininity (for if not rebellious, then what on earth was it doing, dressed up in boy's clothes, carousing round Cambridge with a group of ne'er-do-wells like himself and Bankes and company?), topped by a long, bony nose, tailed by long bony feet, and with a pair of shoulders on it almost as broad as his own. Did he still want it, he wondered anxiously? Did he even know what to do with it? The choirboy Edleston might well have been his ideal of manhood, but the Miss Edleston who had replaced him was about as far removed from his ideal of womanhood as it was possible to be. Living away from her family; skirmishing; swimming; biffing people with paper-weights — the very idea of a young girl behaving in such an unladylike fashion made him shudder. An Amazon, that was what he had unwittingly attached himself to; a hoyden. And what on earth was he to do, if you please, with a five-foot ten-inch hoyden?

As he lay wondering, however, the hoyden belched again and opened her eyes, and his perplexities dissolved on the instant. In a way he had never done before (or, better, in the very same way that he had always done before — with little Mary Duff as a child, with the exquisite Margaret Parker, with his cousin the other Mary, with the former Edleston and with any and every living thing that had spoken directly to his heart; in the same way, only to a different degree, a hundred times stronger, as if all his fragmentary flirts and passions had rolled themselves in a twinkling into one wholly satisfactory, homogenous bundle), he fell in love.

As if immediately aware of this on his own account, and a lot more besides, Edleston flushed scarlet and his hands flew to his chest to cover it. That is: the fair Miss Edleston blushed and her hands flew to her breasts to cover them. But, quicker than she, he covered them for her with his face and held the hands tightly in his own: 'Witch,' he murmured into the damp shirt, hardly able to restrain his laughter, 'devious creature and deplorable swimmer that you are, I have found you out.'

'About time too,' said Miss Edleston faintly (if this indeed was her name), 'I was beginning to think you never would.'

Anna yawned. As far as she could see the latest adjustments to the program had not heightened its interest in the opposite sex at all, but had merely made it introspective. It had answered her questions about the brothel — or about the 'establishment' as it preferred to term it — with polite but short answers such as: AN EXPENSIVE BUT INSTRUCTIVE EXPERIENCE, ALL THINGS CONSIDERED, or (for it was of course the Professor's code number that she was using), WHY DO YOU WANT TO KNOW? HAVE YOU NEVER VISITED ONE YOURSELF? And when pressed it had come up with a flummoxing: LATER, IF YOU DON'T MIND. THAT IS THE SORT OF TOPIC I ONLY DISCUSS IN DETAIL WHEN I AM DRUNK.

But after this, as if tired of being interrogated, it had switched over to its 'browsing' mode in which position it had anchored itself resolutely for the past half hour, resisting all her efforts to lead it back into conversation, and countering any direct attempt to switch it back on to 'input/output' by writing on the screen the touching request: IMPLORO PACE — which was almost impossible for her not to grant.

There seemed therefore little she could do but sit and watch the printer as she was doing now, and hope for a spontaneous change of mood. It did not make interesting watching. Every so often the pace would quicken slightly and a dot or squiggle appear amid the blankness, and just recently she had caught sight of the entire word 'NINCOMPOOP' followed by a row of no less than six exclamation marks. But these were isolated flashes. In the main the printer seemed to have settled itself into a comfortable groove, its carriage swinging rhythmically over the empty paper, backwards and forwards, covering just over half the width of the page each time. In fact from the briefness and regularity of the motion, Anna had begun to suspect that the computer was quoting poetry to itself, under its breath as it were, and that this was the reason for its absorption.

Although she rather missed its chatter, she was reluctant to disturb it: the language — what little it had used — seemed to her well-balanced now and neither scurrilous *nor* straitlaced in spite of what the male assistant had predicted. But she knew that the assistants, both of them, once they realized what had happened would want to chivvy the machine back into a more sociable frame of mind: they were always very keen on maintaining what they called 'maximum semantic productivity'.

She waited another moment, to give the computer a little more time for whatever it was about, and then called to them. 'I'm afraid it's gone into a bit of a brown study. At present it seems to be declaiming invisible verses. Is there anything we can do to stop it?'

12 And Memoirs Less Proper

'. . . When two pure hearts are pour'd in one another
And love too much, and yet can not love less;
But almost sanctify the sweet excess,
By the immortal wish and power to bless.'

It was a pleasure how he could reel it off without so
much as a note before him.

'Mix'd in each other's arms and heart in heart
etc . . . etc . . .'

Don Juan, Canto the Fourth. Because it was *Don Juan*
they ought to be looking into if they wanted to know
the secret of his great love, not those mournful dirges to
the departed Thyrza. There, after all, was where he had
set it all out — or tried to: in the sad little story of Juan
and Haidée. There, wrapped in the layers of some of his
funniest and most satirical writing, hidden like a tear-
drop in a pipe of claret (and what better place for the
concealment of a tear-drop, pray, unless it be the bath
water?), lay the most sincere portrayal of requited and
fulfilled love that he had ever attempted to set to paper.
Sincere because true; true because felt; felt because
sincere. The innocence of the young lovers; their discovery of one another; the flowering of carnal passion
between them unsullied by moral strictures or hypocrisy; the timeless, flawless world in which they find
themselves transported — everything, every scene and

every detail, from the waterlogged meeting of the lovers by the shore, down to the irate father, Lambro's, intrusion on their paradise and their brutal return to earth, had been taken — save for the odd flourish or two here and there — from life.

And from death, of course; from death as well. He had never again felt that sense of complete well-being in love: Caroline Lamb too wild and waspish, Lady O too worn; Augusta too pillowy, Annabella not half pillowy enough; Teresa too female, and Loukas besides being at the opposite extreme of things too male, simply too distant and himself too tired.

Although sometimes with Loukas, in the last days in Greece when he had watched the boy sleeping off his fever, or when they had ridden out together in the early mornings before the rains came and the roads got so bad, just an echo of the feeling had come back to him: faint, but strong enough to remind him that he had once felt it.

Love? Who knows? There was little shared about it; it was more like an inspired selfishness. You started off as two people, and somewhere along the way, by some trick of alchemy or magic, a merger came about so complete that — abracadabra and hey presto — once it was accomplished it was yourself you ended up loving. Which was most likely what you wanted to do all along. So . . . love? Self-love? Did it matter which? At any rate, in the span of his six and thirty years he had felt it in Alba's company alone, and whether it had been for Alba herself or for the George Gordon, Ld Byron, who dwelt inside her at that particular time as she in him, didn't really signify.

Alba. Yes, Alba; that was the name. Not, as she would have people believe, a Mr John Edleston, charming, well-spoken choirboy of obscure origins,

140

chaperoned by an aunt, gracing himself with a little musical education before settling down to the life of a merchant in the metropolis. Not even a Miss Edleston of similar stamp. But, as he learned later, Alba of the awesome and unmentionable surname; blue-stockinged, pig-headed scion of one of the foremost reigning houses in the whole of Europe; chaperoned not by an aunt but by a terrified English governess-cum-lady-in-waiting; helping herself furtively to a pinch of academic snuff before knuckling down to her royal duties in her homeland.

The truth of all this, and its dire implications for their future together, had come out in stages. In Cambridge there had been little time to talk. In the first place Alba had been due to leave almost immediately, and although she succeeded in putting off her departure for a fortnight or so – just long enough for him to purchase the famous bear for her as an engagement present – in the end there had been no more bamboozling the governess; a brother had arrived in London, letters had been despatched, and she had had to leave. In the second place, during the few precious weeks that had remained they had been too busy with other things to spare much time for conversation. Understandably enough.

Later, though, in the days of their elopement when they had hidden away in rented rooms in Brompton – ('Compromise me, Byron,' she had urged, 'it's the only way we have left now of getting my father's consent'; often as not followed languidly by, 'Compromise me again'; and he who hated compromise, how eager he had been to comply); or, later still, when in a last desperate attempt to find somebody to marry them before it was too late they had fled to Brighton with her brother the *Principe Furioso* hot on their heels, and taken rooms there; *then* they had found time for talking

141

all right. They had laid on the uncomfortable strange beds in the uncomfortable strange rooms, and as happily ensconced as cherubim on clouds, had talked away for days on end. Dreams, memories, respective childhoods, foibles, likes, dislikes – whatever came into their heads, and whatever was in there already, it had all come out; until by the end of it there was hardly a detail of Alba's existence that he didn't know as well as his own. Years after, on his travels, he had visited one of the houses she had stayed in as a child and he had been able to recognize it not by the name or the location, but by a description she had given him then of a game of hide-and-seek played in the grounds there one summer with her cousins when she was six. (And even though many years had passed, as soon as he recognized the building you could bet he had left it smartly enough for fear of being identified.) She had told him about the succession of English nurses and governesses whose language she ended up speaking almost better than her own; about how she had yearned to see the places they used to speak of. 'Oxford, Cambridge, Bath, Edinburgh, Bishop's Stortford . . .' 'Bishop's Stortford? Are you sure?' Yes, she was: one of her favourite governesses had come from Bishop's Stortford and had painted it to her in the most glowing terms. 'Ah well then,' he promised, 'we will visit it one day when we have time'; she had explained how she had longed to drink tea ('No regrets?' 'No regrets') and to taste the mysterious-sounding dishes they seemed one and all to hanker after with such nostalgia ('Still no regrets?' 'Still no *real* regrets'); how she had desired above all else to study at university, and how she had starved herself to the verge of death in order to get her father to agree to the incredible scheme she had devised for doing so.

'Wasn't it a little tricky to wangle the actual enrolment?' he'd asked.

'Oh no, not for a family like mine. We are a very resourceful lot. Once it was decided that I should go they set about the thing in style. I'm not sure the Pope wasn't approached at one moment,' and she gave a funny little nod, half-proud, half-mocking. 'Hasn't it ever struck you as odd that as a mere choirboy I should be a fully-fledged student, be let off choir practice whenever I feel like it, and proceed to my degree *tamquam nobiles*?'

'I'd never thought about it,' he'd said.

And of course he hadn't. That was the trouble. But as they'd lain there under cover of the willow, 'mix'd in each other's arms and heart in heart' to put it politely, with the voices of Hobhouse and the others and the splash of their oars coming to them fitfully through the leaves ('They can't be far. Could have sworn they went thisaway. Byron! Edleston! Where have you got to?' and fainter, 'Oh let 'em be, Hobby. No coming to grief on a day like this. Don't pester. Don't fuss. You're as bad as an old nurse'), who could have dwelt on such minor details as names or parentage? All he had thought to ask was the Christian name; and when he learnt it the fountain of laughter and happiness which had been welling up in him since the moment he had made his remarkable discovery shot up like a geyser, expelling all his bile and melancholy with it. Alba! He could have shouted it aloud. Perhaps he did. Alba. The dawn. The sun rising on his life. He, the lame diffident boy, cursed from the cradle with deformity, saddled with a mortgaged estate, a harpy of a mother, a tendency to run to fat and a splenetic vision which enabled him to see the black side of everything, was suddenly basking in ray after ray of resplendent sunshine. He was in love. With a *woman*. And she was in love with him. Not only this, but his beloved was young and clever and slender and – due allowance made for her size – beautiful, and for the time being at any rate so was he. They were made for one another; meant for one another; destined for one another. The trifling little obstacle to a perfect fit which had so far impeded their union . . . (Wait a minute. Trifling? When it had been hovering over him in his dreams like a column of basalt, turning them all to nightmares?) . . . Well, anyway, trifling or not it had been planed away in a trice, seeing that it had never really existed in the first place, and now at last they were free to love each other as both of them had always wanted from the very start.

Perhaps he *should* have waited – at least for the surname. Perhaps they should have held back – bide a wee, bide a wee, as they said in Scotland. But then again, they were so young, and had waited so long already. Or perhaps they should have managed their affairs quite differently, spoken to one another at length, learnt about each other's families, carried out the necessary formalities, submitted themselves to an official engagement, awaited – horror upon horrors – their respective comings of age; and perhaps had they done so, the ending too would have been different. But *à quoi bon*, it had seemed at the time, when their love was already so complete? At all events, she, who knew how things stood, did not care; and he, who cared, did not know; and they had set about each other like tigers there and then, with no further preliminaries, under the leaves of the willow, within earshot of Hobhouse and his crew, with never a thought as to whether it was wise or prudent or advisable. It was necessary to both, and that was all.

Afterwards, sweating, surprised, flecked with pieces of grass; Alba still belching slightly now and again, his weight on her stomach seeming to have brought up another little remnant or two of river water, they lay together in the shade and looked at one another. Alba was the first to speak.

'If this is all there is to it,' she said, 'oh, excuse me. If this is all there is to it, then I don't see what you were so worried about. We could have got it over sooner. I was not in a position to know, of course, but I never imagined it was such a quick transaction as this, or,' her hand edged its way between their stomachs in exploration, 'such an untidy one. Otherwise . . .'

He looked down on her in utter contentment, kissing her mouth shut. 'It needn't be either, believe me, Alba. This was for duty: not a good example to go by. Some people do it comfortably, you know, in beds, for pleasure. They take their time about it, too. It's quite a well-know fact.'

Her face twitched, unconvinced.

'What if I gave you another example?'

'When?' was all she asked, without much curiosity.

He smiled. 'As soon as I am able to find a suitable one.'

'And when will that be?'

'I don't know,' he said honestly. He put a finger to his lips and listened for a second as if trying to capture some imperceptible sound. 'But I'm not sure I don't feel like looking for one straight away.'

Later still, when the banks of the river had become grey and misty and all sounds about them had ceased, save for the bells in the distance and the scurrying of the odd water-hen amongst the lilies, they lay, rather more quietly now, and talked at greater length.

'Not half bad, Mr Edleston. If you will please always

145

to wear a shirt and trousers in future: I can get at you so much more easily.'

Alba squinted down at what she could see of her dishevelled clothing. 'If you will please to get at me. I see there may well be more to this pastime than I thought.' She stretched under him and gave a yawn. 'Do you remember – that day when you told us about your initiation at Madame What's-her-name's? I think it was that that must have put me off. It sounded so terrible – all those poor women, paid to cry out and wriggle and pretend they were enjoying themselves. Not paid very handsomely either, from what you said. Didn't you even claim a discount at the end?'

'I was *given* a discount,' he said, pushing the end of the long ivory nose upwards to see what it would look like shorter. 'And it wasn't meant to sound terrible, it was meant to sound funny. It sounded terrible to *you* because you were jealous, that's why. And it serves your right: if you had told me the truth about yourself I'd never have gone there. I only went because of you.'

'But I tried to tell you the truth,' she said indignantly, 'and when you wouldn't listen I tried to show you. But you were so cold and so fierce that I gave up. You told me I was behaving like a pig, if you remember. My pride would not allow me to go further. I thought to myself: well, that's that; if ever he is to have me now it must be because he's so far gone that he no longer cares whether I am a man or a woman, or what I am. So the fault is yours, not mine.'

'Pride is a bad counsellor,' he teased. 'And a *stuck* pig, for your information, is not a metaphoric-ally swinish animal but merely a noisy one. Not care whether you were a man or a woman indeed! I never heard such a piece of arrant and utterly female

146

nonsense. On such exacting terms you might well have lost me altogether; I might never have come back; I very nearly didn't.'

He propped himself up on his elbows to ease her of his weight and they looked at one another and laughed.

'I'm glad you did.'

'*I'm* glad I did. Anyway,' he went on, 'whoever's fault it was, one way and another I'm not sure we didn't benefit from my experience. I was rather pleased with this second foray — thought I came out of it rather well, didn't you? See how long the shadows have grown? We must have been at it a couple of hours, if not more.'

'Two hours!' said Alba, struggling free and sitting up in alarm. 'That means I've gone and missed evensong again. Bother.' And she began tucking her shirt back into her trousers.

But before she could finish, he had plunged his hands inside the shirt-front again and placed them possessively over the telltale breasts. 'Please don't put them away just yet,' he begged. 'Let me say good evening to them nicely first. And while I am about my salutations you could perhaps tell me a few little things about their owner. True things,' he warned her, punctuating his words by a gentle nibble, first at one breast, then at the other, 'like what her name is, where she comes from, what on earth she thinks she's doing cavorting around dressed up as a choirboy and driving poor students like myself to distraction, and whether at her earliest convenience she will condescend to marry an impoverished but quite respectable nobleman of promising . . . Keep still. Stop wriggling so. You said you didn't hold with wriggling. You've *missed* your singing appointment, so it's no good . . .'

'That's just what I was thinking. It's no good hurrying.'

147

'Oh Alba, Alba! I thought you'd read books on anatomy.'

'Sssh,' she whispered, drawing him close. 'You can't always go by books.'

Which was why it was not until darkness had fallen and they were padding back barefoot together over the grass to recover the other half of their clothes, shivering, clinging to each other for warmth and laughing and chattering like children after a wicked but successful escapade, that they finally got round to the surname.

It came as something of a shock to him. And once the shock had worn off (for the unexpected reversal of rank, although humiliating to begin with, had its bright side: it was always a good thing to marry blood, he couldn't help thinking. *And* money. Especially when you hadn't particularly been looking for either), it took him quite some time to understand what the surname meant. In terms, that is, of obstacles to be overcome.

'What do you mean, a *mésalliance*?'

Alba was silent.

'Marriage to a peer of England a *mésalliance*? I can't think any parents in their right minds would consider it that. And once they learn that I am of royal descent *myself* on the Scottish side?'

Alba still said nothing.

'But you *must* marry me now,' he urged, amused, chiding, pinching her at intervals, totally unable to share her seriousness. 'It's the only way I can ever hope to recover that expensive jewel I gave you.' And then, falling to his knees and addressing the heavens in mock despair, 'Behold the blessings of a lucky lot: the bridegroom willing but the lady not.'

Getting no response to his clowning, however, he stood up again, took her by the shoulders and spun her round to face him. 'I'll talk to them, Alba,' he said, becoming serious now, and using all the confidence at his command, which was still a considerable amount at that stage. 'You just wait and see. I'm very good at getting people to do what I want.'

In reply Alba gave a great shiver and clung to him hard, and he wrapped his arms round her and rubbed her as he would a horse. Fool that he was, he thought she was shivering from cold.

'Well, that's it. Nice work, Anna. I'm sure we're all very grateful to you for your help.' It was the Professor in person, a wine glass in one hand and a carton of fizzy Italian white wine in the other, getting ready to celebrate the end of the language-checking phase. 'My assistants are satisfied. I'm satisfied. And,' here he glanced a little nervously in Anna's direction, 'I take it you're satisfied yourself as well.' Following the correction of the parameters on heterosexuality, a further hour and a half of everyone's evening leisure time had just been spent at her suggestion on overhauling the program's notions of social behaviour, and as time progressed the Professor and his helpers had begun to wilt as markedly as the flowers.

'Not that you didn't have a point there about rank, though,' he conceded. 'I'd noticed myself that it was a bit lax about titles. Never bothered to address me as "Professor" that I recall.'

Anna shook her head. 'I don't think it will do that even now, you know,' she said, rather hoping that the computer would bear her out in this. 'You must remember that dons and professors and such like would have held more or less the status of superior servants in Byron's eyes. No, what we've given the program is an increased awareness of purely *social* standing. Gentry,

149

nobility, royalty; that sort of thing. The idea is that if ever the program gets too absorbed in itself, the user can regain its interest by flaunting a title. I don't think it's cheating really. Byron himself could be a terrible old snob at times.'

The Professor grunted. 'And it works?'

'Yes,' said Anna, gathering her papers together and turning away from the terminal with a sigh. 'At least it's certainly been much more forthcoming with me now that I've introduced myself as Lady Anna. I think it's given it the final touch as far as the language is concerned. There may be the odd word now and again that needs substituting, but the general tone seems to me hard to improve on. It's funny,' she sighed again, 'sometimes, particularly when it's not being technical, it's so convincing that I can fancy myself talking to the actual flesh and blood Byron.' She paused and, glancing back at the computer, managed to ask something that had been on her mind for quite a while. 'Do you think I could keep some of the print-outs — the ones you don't want — so as to have something to remember it by when I'm gone?'

'Afraid not,' said the Professor, biting into the carton with his teeth and humming as he poured out the wine. 'Afraid not.' Then he caught sight of Anna's face as he handed her her glass and appeared to change his mind. 'Oh all right,' he said, not unkindly, 'I suppose you can go ahead and take what you like. As long as you take it in photocopy, that is, and leave us the originals. There's this historian from Cambridge turning up tomorrow, as no doubt you've heard, and he'll most likely want to go through all the recent stuff with a toothcomb. Particularly the parts about the university in Byron's time — I'm told you got some quite interesting copy out of it on that.'

150

'Yes,' said Anna, 'but not as much as I'd have liked. I got on to a very interesting track at one point, but I had to leave it. I wish I'd had more time.'

'Time!' said the Professor sweepingly, raising his glass, 'we all need more time, and time is what we none of us have. Tomorrow you'll be back in your university. And by the way,' he remembered to add, 'do tell your colleagues there from me how glad we were that they could spare you for so long. Next week we three shall be off to Los Angeles to introduce LB to a group of critical rivals who will do their best to scuttle him for us — LA, meet LB they'll expect me to say, no doubt.' He waited for Anna's smile which was not forthcoming. 'And the week after we'll have got him off our chests altogether and'll be starting on another program.'

'Ah,' said Anna, not realizing her mistake until the question was out of her mouth, 'and whose brain will it be next time?' Without meaning to she had evidently touched on a subject of great contention. The Professor took the question from her nimbly, turned it to his assistants, and then, in the uncomfortable silence that followed, went on to answer it loudly himself, his voice booming at his colleagues over the rim of his glass.

There followed a long tirade, most of which Anna was unable to follow, although the words themselves were quite clear. 'Not so much "whose" brain, then, as "what's", ' was the conclusion. 'No more poets or men of letters. No more chatterboxes or' — with a jerk of the head towards the computer — 'boxes full of chatter. The road lies elsewhere. We must make for the core. Fewer and more basic symbols. That's the key.' The Professor paused to give full effect to his words. 'What we want to work on next is a grasshopper's brain or an earthworm's.'

'Fine,' said his female assistant, meeting the challenge

with an unusual show of spirit. 'And where are the funds to come from, may I ask? From the Royal Association of Grasshopper Breeders?' At her elbow the second assistant giggled.

The Professor ignored him. 'Funds or no funds, that's not the point,' he went on unsmilingly. 'The point is, that I see *no* point in churning out yet another expensive failure on the lines of this one.' And with a thump he brought his glass down on the terminal, spilling the wine.

There was a silence. Anna looked worriedly from face to face and began to mop up the liquid with her handkerchief. 'Failure?' she asked, wondering if she could have heard correctly. 'But it's not a *failure* surely? I mean . . . how can you think that Albè's a failure? Oh, I know he's been a bit shirty sometimes, and some of the time he's unco-operative, and some of the time he's bored; but we've cleared that up surely now? And anyway it only goes to show how successful he is, how like a real brain, how like . . .'

Realizing, however, that no one was listening to her but that all were hovering instead on the brink of what promised to be a long and heated argument, she added the 'Byron' quietly to herself, finished her drying of the spilt wine, and sat down again at the terminal. She knew only too well now that there was little change to be got out of the machine on Thyrza; but all the same there were a couple of other little things in Byron's life which she wanted to ask it about while she still had the chance. The destroyed memoirs, for example. Except that it would take too long. Or the reason why Byron had to leave England so urgently in 1809 — 'Quit the country I must immediately' he had written at the time in a letter to his agent or someone. Or else she might ask it for a few more details about the shadowy Miss

Cameron, whom he had lived with briefly in rooms in Brompton; taken to Brighton with him, dressed up as a boy; and whom, despite the dismissive way he had referred to her in his correspondence (which as she well knew by now never carried much weight as far as Byron's true opinions were concerned) he seemed to have been on the point of actually marrying — before the inevitable bust-up between them, that was. There again it was the poetry that gave the clue.

> *Remind me not, remind me not,*
> *Of those beloved, those vanish'd hours,*
> *When all my soul was given to thee . . .*

All my soul? He wouldn't have written to the girl like that, would he, unless she'd meant a good deal more to him than he let on to his friends at the time? She listened for a moment to the argument that was going on behind her. It seemed already to be waning slightly: there would only be time for one question. Which should it be then: Cameron, or reason for leaving England? Departure, she decided. Quick, before anyone noticed, let her just ask it why Byron left England in such a hurry in 1809.

13 Reminiscing

The very same question Shelley put to him that evening
in Ravenna. 'But why did you have to leave England
like that, in such a rattling hurry? Hadn't it all quiet-
ened down by then?' Only it wasn't evening; it was
getting on for dawn more like, and they were both of
them more than a little drunk.

The evening had begun badly. Shelley had arrived
late — hungry, nervous, out of sorts, armed with a
written list of disagreeable topics to be discussed
between them (topics such as his, Byron's, parental
responsibilities towards Allegra, her maintenance and
education, and what was to be done about muzzling
that b——h of a mother of hers) which he kept folding
and unfolding as he tucked into his food and did not
relinquish until he finally found a suitable place for it
under one of the plates.

To begin with, in the jerky, unsatisfactory way that
he'd noticed scribblers nearly always had of speaking
to one another about their profession, particularly in a
case like this when their knowledge of each other's
public mind outran that of the private, they had talked
of their work: of what writings they were currently
engaged on, what had happened to the stuff already
written, what, if anything, they were planning to write
next. (And he couldn't help noticing that Shelley was
cagey over this last point, as he knew himself to have

154

been over the second to last.) Next, Shelley still busy with his food, and he himself plying them both with beakers of the local wine to try and brighten the atmosphere a little, they had shifted to critics and publishers. But to little avail: grumble, grumble; grouse, grouse; and Shelley chewing away so noisily that it seemed he hadn't had a square meal put before him in months. Which, given the Spartan tenor of Mrs Shelley's housekeeping, he had reminded himself as he watched, was probably the case. Poor Shelley. All those terrible raw-fruit puddings and that husk-ridden bread. No wonder the fellow was so stringy. He had forgotten, of course, since the last time they had met, what a hard man Shelley was to relax with: how, even when eating — as he was now, with a vengeance — he always sat on the edge of his chair, never in the middle, and how he danced around with his legs all the time. It was as bad as trying to converse with an overwound clockwork puppet. Shelley's own circle, he seemed to remember, described this restlessness of his as 'mercurial', an offshoot of his genius; to him it seemed merely annoying.

As the evening wore on, however, what with the food and the wine, and in part thanks to a cool night breeze which stirred itself into motion around midnight after a day of punishing heat and stillness, they had grown slowly happier in each other's company. So much so, in fact, that when the time had come for discussing the dreaded personal matters — in theory the object of Shelley's visit and normally the cause of much embarrassment between them — Shelley's charge had run down almost completely and they had found themselves both lolling quite peacefully in their chairs, smiling at one another in comfortable silence like oldish, if not old, friends.

155

Just for a moment Shelley's eyes had flickered to the dish which concealed the list, but had then darted back mischievously to his own, and they had smiled again, like conspirators, over the flame of the candle. 'Later, Shelley,' he said lazily, stretching out and taking him by the sleeve. 'Come and see my menagerie, while the servants clear away — if they're still up, that is, the sluggards. Now is the time of day I usually give the crow his bath. I've rigged up a kind of bottle with a squirter so that I can spray him under the wings. You'll see how he loves it. The eagle now doesn't seem to take to it in the same way, nor does the crane or the falcon; but then the heat doesn't seem to flatten them quite so bad as it does my poor crow. Come on, come and watch.'

Although taken aback at first by the number and variety of beasts in the collection, Shelley had watched the nightly sprinkling ceremony with an interest that had bordered on delight.

'I think I could do with the same sort of treatment myself,' he had sighed when it was over, holding wide his arms. 'Wine for the inside, water for the out.' And they had ended up by spraying themselves liberally — capering round the room in the midst of the drowsy animals, tripping over wings and tails and laughing their heads off — and by swallowing yet another litre or so of Recioto wine, progressing as they did so from friendship to brotherhood. If, indeed, the latter could be considered the closer tie.

It was then, or shortly afterwards, that they had embarked on the confessions, passing in review in unfettered tipsy candour present companions (a bit of a grumble here, too); future conquests (non-existent as far as he was concerned, but Shelley full of enterprise, being younger); past loves and past mistakes (of which

156

plenty on both sides). Finally — *dulcis in fundo* — Shelley had gone over the business of the illegitimate child he was alleged to have abandoned in the Naples orphanage. (Not a very pretty story, by the way, but not half so discreditable to Shelley as that Swiss heifer of a Consul's wife went around trying to make out.) And he, in return for the confidence, or because he had never told anyone the full story and wanted to get it off his chest, or perhaps merely because he knew the story would appeal to Shelley and he felt like telling it, had capped Shelley's confession by regaling him with the entire, unexpurgated history of his secret love for Alba.

The story, as he knew it would, had tickled Shelley's fancy no end. Hence his now badgering for more details. 'But why did you have to leg it like that, Byron?' he asked, repeating his question about the departure. 'That's what I want to know.'

(Of course. It was what everyone had wanted to know at the time: Hanson, his mother, his friends, even Fletcher and Hobhouse who were leaving with him. He could remember the anxious days spent in Falmouth, waiting for a wind to get up and the packet-boat to depart, and how he had expected at every moment to feel a hand clamp down on his shoulder and a piece of steel skewer him from behind. 'What's all the haste in aid of, Byron? Relax, for goodness' sake, enjoy yourself.' 'What are you fretting about, M'Lord? The wind'll come when it comes. Your storming around the place like that won't make it come any faster.' Neither Hobhouse nor Fletcher had understood his nervousness, his longing to be off. But then, neither Hobhouse nor Fletcher was to know there was a band of assassins out to kill him; a foreign power determined to wipe him off the face of the earth. That, he had wanted to tell

157

them, was what the hurry was in aid of. That was what entitled him to feel a little jumpy.

But fear hadn't been the only reason for his departure, he could see that now. Part of him, it was true, had been running for safety. And part of him had been running just for the sake of running somewhere new. But another part of him — perhaps, looking back on it, the most important part of all — was beyond matters of survival or adventure by then. It was dead already; had died at the moment of his parting with Alba, and was taking itself to sea for burial. This, however, was something that Shelley might not understand, and anyway he had no particular desire to tell him.)

'Why? Because they was *furriners*. Hot-blooded,' he replied, and giggled into his glass. For now that he had at last dug it up and told it aloud for somebody else's benefit, he could see that the story did have an irresistibly funny side to it.

Shelley stuck out a long, bony leg and squinted amiably at his foot. 'You mean you were frightened they would call you out? But I thought you said you'd already fought a duel.'

'With the *brother*, Shelley. You haven't been paying attention. We eloped to Brighton, Alba disguised as my groom. We lodged in a hotel there, Alba no longer disguised as my groom, which would have looked rather odd seeing that we shared a room, but as my doxy, the disreputable Miss Cameron. The brother followed us to Brighton, tracked us down, challenged me, and I fought a duel with him there. Nothing much came of the duel, apart from a few scratches, so perhaps the family didn't consider itself appeased. *This* time — the second time — it was a kind of execution squad sent by Papa.'

Shelley hiccoughed and patted his stomach. 'All that

158

length of time later? How long was it since they'd spirited her away, did you say?'

He counted carefully on his fingers. 'Well, let me see. It was July when the brother ran us to ground — he was a delightful man, you know, Shelley, the brother. In any other circumstances I think we'd have become friends — and it was April or thereabouts when I first heard that the vendetta expedition was under way. So — roughly nine months.'

'Nine months? Nine *months*? Oh, ho, ho,' said Shelley, he too fighting something of a losing battle with his giggles. 'You don't think by any chance . . . ? I mean nine months is a curious stretch of time. You don't think', and he snorted outright into his wine, blowing bubbles, 'that the august personage had perhaps become a *Grand*papa in the meantime, and that that was what he was so incensed about?'

He considered Shelley's question, frowning in mock seriousness. 'Unlikely,' he said at last. 'You see we used — how shall I put it? — a famous *Greek* remedy against fertility. And an excellent remedy it was, too,' he added. 'I remember I tried to convince my wife, Lady Byron, of its efficacy once, and you never *saw* such fireworks! Believe me, Shelley, if it hadn't been for the noise I'd have made on my way there, I think she'd have gladly seen me to the gallows for it. Which only goes to show', he went on chewing pensively on a thumbnail, 'how different women can be; because, believe it or not, the remedy was Alba's own idea.' He leaned forward, anxious to impress this on his listener. 'She *discovered* it,' he explained proudly. 'Thought it up for herself. The ears, Byron, she told me in all seriousness, would do every bit as well in theory, but they are too small!'

'Eureka!' said Shelley, his battle lost, dabbing helplessly at his eyes. 'Some discovery. I don't believe a word.'

'And why not, may I ask?'

'Because it's too good to be true: a royal princess dressed up as a choirboy, beautiful as Antinous, wise as Athena, and with the flair of a Newton in the bedchamber! You're making the whole thing up.'

Nettled, he leant forward and grabbed hold of Shelley's boot, twisting it sideways. 'What a way to receive a confidence,' he fired at him. 'How dare you doubt me. Every word I've told you is true. Say you believe me, or I'll twist your leg off.'

'Very well, I believe you, I believe you,' Shelley conceded after a half-hearted struggle to straighten both foot and face. 'At least I promise to do my best not to disbelieve. But tell me more. You said she died. What did she die of? From what you say she must have been a tough young lady. Not the sort to come to an early demise. Didn't it ever cross your mind that she might have been deliberately put out of the way, to keep her from running off again and rejoining you?'

(Didn't it ever cross his mind? What *hadn't* crossed his mind in those miserable days? He had imagined Alba locked in a battle of wills with her inflexible relatives. Imagined her incarcerated, beaten, tortured, humiliated, starving herself to death again like as not, only this time with a more bitter kind of success awaiting her at the end. Pig-headedness seemed to run in the family; there was no telling what lengths her adversaries would go to to thwart her, or she to overcome their resistance and get her own way. Imprisonment, punishment, attempted escape, defiance, even despair − all of these possibilities had crossed his mind, and crossed it moreover like a convoy of ploughs or harrows.

News of what actually had happened had not caught up with him until he and Hobhouse had reached Turkey, and he could remember that his first reaction on reading the letter which contained the news — presumably it had been sent by the brother, although there was no signature, just a seal imprinted triumphantly at the foot of the page — was relief that she was still alive. Then he had re-read the message and taken it in, and had felt nothing at all: only the heat beating down on his head and a sudden disinclination to breathe.

'I'm afraid I must make our excuses to the Ambassador,' he had managed to say quite coherently to Hobhouse, who was standing by watching. They had been due to dine at the Embassy that evening. 'I don't think I feel quite adapted for society in my present mood.'

'Oh,' said Hobhouse, studying him carefully, disappointment over the ambassadorial dinner slowly giving way to alarm. 'Why? What has happened? Have you received bad news from England?' Then, with a disconcerting flash of insight, 'It's Edleston, isn't it, Byron? That's what the letter is about: something has happened to Edleston.'

He had been too taken off his guard to deny outright, and had had to fob Hobby off with a story of some scandal or other in which the imaginary Edleston was involved. How he had managed to think it up on the spur of the moment, with the pain he was in, he did not know. But it was often like that with him: the sharper the pain, the sharper the wits.)

Abruptly he let go of Shelley's foot. 'Poison, you mean?' he said. 'Daggers and whatnot? No, I can't say that it did. Such measures weren't even necessary as things turned out, because the moment the father got her back he married her off smartly to some Hunnish

161

princeling or other. A cousin, I think it was. And curiously enough, so I was told later, the marriage was quite a success while it lasted. Not that they wouldn't have resorted to both expedients without so much as a blink, but they didn't have to: they simply extracted her word from her that she would never attempt to see or contact me ever again – how I do not know; I only know that the speed with which they extracted it hurt and angered me at the time: I suppose I had been expecting her to put up more of a fight – and that was that.' He closed his eyes and added softly, 'An envelope with some hair in it was awaiting me on my return, you know – about the same length and colour. I liked to think it was from her – I still like to think so. But of course,' and he opened his eyes and shook his head with a smile, 'it could have come from anyone. Women were always sending me snippets of their hair in those days. If I'd kept all the tresses I've received over the years I could have stuffed a mattress with them by now. She was dead, anyway, by the time I opened the envelope. She died in the spring of 1811, roughly a year after her marriage, although I didn't hear about her death until months after, when I was back in England. It was phthisis she died of, I believe, or one of those other things that I can never spell.'

'Or pronounce.'

'Hark at the scholar! *Or* pronounce.'

('She died in May of phthisis.' Seven syllables, or eight if you stuck to 'consumption', which was perhaps wiser. A lapidary formula which he had chosen never to examine very closely, and to expand only in the highly literary form of his poetry where the dictates of craftsmanship managed to neutralize it very success-fully for him. Death, in any case, had added little to his loss.

The final message had come to him at Newstead — one thing you could say for royalty being that they at least had the good grace to publicize their births and marriages and deaths and various goings-on — and he had taken it very calmly. For a few days, as a precaution against the image of Alba's face which would keep appearing before him in a ghostly and disconsolate way, he had got himself thoroughly and regularly drunk; later, chiefly out of deference towards his liver, he had even taken a short trip to Cambridge. But neither of these expedients had been strictly necessary: the image had begun to fade of its own accord, and Cambridge had presented him with nothing but a leafless willow tree, an empty Chapel undergoing repairs, and a curt refusal from the present occupant of his old rooms when he had asked to be allowed in to revisit them. So truthfully the news of Alba's death had come as a stonemason's afterthought — a slab to cover a grave already dug.)

Shelley's voice interrupted this melancholy train of thought. 'And the cornelian heart?' he asked, implying that he still couldn't believe entirely unless shown something concrete.

'The cornelian? Ah, that's an odd little story. I entrusted it to a lady friend of mine — no, Shelley, *not* the sort of friend you suppose. A true lady, and a true friend — and asked her to keep it for me while I was abroad. I was afraid of losing it on my travels, you see. But I must have worded my request somewhat clumsily, for the lady thought it was for her, that I had intended it as a gift, and said, "Thank you, Byron dear," with the most obliging of smiles and tucked it into her reticule.'

'And you never got it back again?'

'Oh yes I did, eventually. But I had to ask for it, and I

only summoned up courage enough to do so later, when all the memories had faded and I began to need — like you do yourself — some kind of proof that the story wasn't just a story but had really taken place. I've still got it, as a matter of fact, lying around in some box or other. It's broken, though. I broke it shortly after I got it back. A very fitting *post scriptum* to the story, don't you think: a heart lost through clumsiness, broken through the same?'

'Yes,' said Shelley, 'that'll do neatly for a *post scriptum*, but what about the *post post scriptum*? The wronged parent, for example. Did he go on chasing after you even when his daughter was dead? And did he ever catch up with you?'

'Aha,' he said in teasing voice, and took another long swig of wine. 'Almost, but not quite. I think I'll save that up, though, for tomorrow evening. Because you are staying, aren't you?' Under the teasing the question had a faintly pleading ring to it. 'It's a long while since I had the pleasure of some recognizably English conversation. Fletcher's all I can depend on for the present, and he's no good because he's gone all Italian in his speech nowadays. "Have some *thè*, Milord," he said to me the other day. "*Thè*" for 'tea', if you please. And he's taken to drinking it cold, too.' He leant towards his friend appealingly. '*Don't* hasten back to the green fruit brigade, Shelley, I beg of you; they'll manage very well without you for a while.'

Shelley leaned forward likewise, loosened the shirt about his neck and opened his fingers wide to let the breeze through them. 'Ah,' he sighed, 'gauze over the windows: air and no insects. You know, it's the first time I've felt at peace since the summer began.' The butterfly hands folded themselves peaceably over his knees after their airing. 'Yes, I'll stay — of course I'll

164

stay. There's nothing so restful as a house with no women in it, and no children.' Then taking up his wine glass again and holding it to his cheek he went on musingly, 'What would have happened, though, do you suppose . . . I mean what difference do you think it would have made to your life if you had married this Alba of yours? If she hadn't capitulated to her family's wishes and hadn't died, and if you had come back from your travels and gone and carried her off as you intended. Would it have made you any happier, d'you think?'

He looked back at Shelley in silence, intrigued by the question but unwilling to give it a serious answer.

(For the moment of their parting — how unbearably sad it had been. The miserable little room with its smell of camphor, the hastily packed cases, the tray with the half-eaten supper on it, Alba's white, frightened face peeking out from beneath the brim of Fletcher's hat which she had been wearing as part of her disguise — he could see it all as clearly as if he'd been sitting there. More so, in fact, for his eyes were no longer awash with tears as they had been then.

'They cannot divide us like this. We cannot leave each other now.'

'Ssssh, sssh. It will not be for long.'

'If it is for long I shall be sundered. There will be an open, bloody wound inside me which will never heal and never cease to hurt. Tell me it will not happen. Tell me. Promise. Swear.'

'Sssssh, my love, ssssh. It will not be for long.'

'Promise. Swear. Give me your word.'

'You have my pledge. Wear it, keep it safe, believe in me. You know I will be back.'

'Whatever happens?'

'Whatever happens.'

'Even if I am fifty?'

'Even if you are ninety-two and I am ninety-four.'

'Promise?'

'Promise, I promise, I promise.'

He could hear the sounds of their voices, speaking those solemn childish words which only children abide by. He could taste the salt of her tears on her skin as he held her, feel the silk of her hair, the warmth of her body, the marquetry precision with which it fitted against his own. He could remember too the shock as they tore themselves apart; how they had looked at each other disbelievingly as if neither of them had thought it possible. And in the background he could still smell that sickly stench of camphor which he'd never been able to stomach then or since.)

With difficulty, he brought Shelley's face into focus again. 'You got the woman you wanted, didn't you?' he asked quizzingly at length.

'Yes,' said Shelley, 'both.'

'Well then. And what difference did it make to you?'

Shelley shrugged and blew on his fingers again. 'Hmm,' he said lightly, 'I know what you're angling after, but I don't think the comparison holds. I love a *scenata*. I never feel more alive than when somebody is accusing me of something. When the atmosphere around me isn't taut enough I even go and tauten it up for myself sometimes. It's the way I'm made. But with you it's different: your life may have been full of upsets, but I don't think myself that you went looking for them. I think that at the bottom of your nature you like routine and quiet and things in their proper places. Take the windows, for example; *I*'ve hardly ever stayed long enough in a house to make it worthwhile netting the windows. Aren't I right? Mightn't marriage to Alba have saved you a lot of heartache and bother?'

166

'Perhaps,' he answered slowly. He poured out the last dregs of the wine for his guest and himself, and sipping on it thoughtfully, felt the parabola of his tipsiness take a dip towards sobriety and then begin to climb again. 'Perhaps, yes, things *would* have been better, all told. But then, as you well know, cause and effect tend to become jumbled in retrospect. There is a void inside me, Shelley, you know. A hunger. A craving. Call it what you will. It made itself felt when I lost Alba, of course it did. But I think it was there before. I think it always was. How far she could have gone towards filling it is anyone's guess. Besides,' he added, rising to his feet, 'I might have made her very unhappy – I have a great talent in that direction.'

They looked at one another and grimaced.

'Anyway, enough of that. It's time we were off to bed,' he tapped lightly on Shelley's outstretched boot. 'Time to get some air on the toes as well as the rest. I'm not sure I'll volunteer to help you myself, after all your travelling, but Fletcher will give you a hand if you like. I'll send him in to you. Oh, by the way, I was forgetting, don't mind the squawks and barks in the morning: the eagle gets a bit peckish for his breakfast sometimes and helps himself to a little *antipasto* off one of the dogs' ears. Myself, I don't usually rise until about two.'

Shelley gave a snakelike wriggle and got to his feet. 'So,' he said yawning, 'reasons of state prevail and the world will never know the secret of Lord Byron's greatest love, nor the true identity of the Thyrza he mourned so disconsolately in his poems. Shame in a way, I suppose,' he considered, 'it would have made up nicely into verse. I bet Murray would have paid you handsomely for it; no quibbling as to guineas or pounds over that one. But there it is. Now no one will ever know who was the real Mr Edleston of the

167

honeyed voice, nor who the real Miss Cameron . . .'

He paused, struck by the name. 'Why Cameron, incidentally?'

'Simple. Cameron — *Decamerone*. It was Alba's choice. I said Dante but she said no, our adventures were more redolent of Boccaccio.'

Shelley smiled. 'Then you do well to keep quiet about them,' he said. 'Imagine your readers learning of an association between Thyrza and Boccaccio. It would not please them at all. They would accuse you of having betrayed your muse.'

He rose and took Shelley by the arm. 'Ah, my muse,' he sighed, 'my lugubrious muse. Wait till they see the latest cantos of the Don, I can hardly be said to have been faithful to it there. Although, if you read carefully, wedged in between the funny bits you will also find a good deal of the melancholy story I have just told you. I don't hold with wasting ideas either. You know,' he added, steering his guest to the doorway, 'you know what my sister once heard a preacher declare in a sermon? "No hopes for them that laughs." I assure you, Shelley, those very words: no hopes for them that laughs. What do you think, could the man have been right?'

But Shelley's reply was lost in the clatter of their feet on the stairs as they made their way to bed, and in the hoots of laughter that accompanied their progress.

14　In Memoriam

The conversation with Shelley had taken place in 1821, when he was thirty-three — hmm, what have these years left to me? Nothing except thirty-three — and now he was . . . what was it? . . . a hundred and ninety-nine. Which had a convenient rhyme in 'mine' if only he could be bothered to think up a fitting couplet, but he couldn't. Couldn't be bothered, that is: for hoary though he might be he was perfectly capable still of writing verse.

It was a curious thing, age. Whenever he'd thought of it before in relation to himself he had always imagined he would wither at the *top* first, like a tree — lose his hair and his teeth and all of the sparkle. Like those firs he'd once seen in the mountains somewhere — grey and dry and sapless, but still standing.

Well, the hair *had* begun to go early, of course, to be quite truthful — before he was even thirty; the moustache had thinned out, blanched; the teeth had stayed on out of courtesy alone. (And in a way he was glad to think that Alba had not been there to watch his decay take place, or he to watch hers. As he had written once with this in mind, 'I know not if I could have borne to see thy beauties fade', and perhaps it was better that he had never been put to the test.) But as regards the sparkle — why, almost two centuries had passed and it was still there. As was the memory, for just look how

169

nifty he was with the quotations. Quite amazing. The very opposite to a tree, in fact: no roots, no trunk or branches, just the top, blossoming away all on its own.

Believe it or not, people were still at him, too, even in this reduced state. Why did you do this? Why did you say that? Did you ever meet so-and-so? Flattering in a way that they were still interested, he supposed, but something of a bore when he couldn't see any of his questioners or make up his mind whether they were worth talking to or not. He had held out on them over the Thyrza/Edleston lark — very properly too: it was none of their business. But perhaps in future it might do to let just a *few* things out of the bag now and again to keep them hopping. It would help while away the time.

Yes, no doubt about it, the top was greener and leafier than ever: it could think, remember, discuss, amuse, lead people on, and even argue with them. What was more (although with less cause for congratulation), it was still able to regret and to feel sadness. For never mind what he had told Shelley that evening, things *would* have been better for him if Alba had lived to marry him. Of course they would. He could see that quite clearly now. For one thing her presence would have kept him out of that muddle with Augusta which he'd only got into in the first place out of loneliness; it might well have helped him steer clear of the lunatic Lamb; and it would most certainly have prevented him from falling into that angular trap laid for him by the Princess of Parallelograms.

Which, Lord only knows, would have been a deliverance. He could remember only too vividly how on his wedding night he had felt the trap clamp down on him; how he had stood there by that great, grim bed with its dusty curtains that had made him sneeze, looking down on Annabella's rosy little pippin face – innocent, healthy, eager to please him but still more pleased with itself; and how, struck perhaps by the colour, the contrast, the pink where there should have been ivory, the brown where there should have been gold, he had been seized by a fit of such longing for Alba and such despair at the life that now lay before him that he had wished himself dead there and then. He had grabbed his pistols, he remembered; turned his back on Annabella, grabbed his pistols, and stormed into the adjoining room with the intent of killing himself on the spot. It had taken Annabella nearly an hour to calm him down and bring him to his senses. Poor Bella: off to a bad start through no fault of her own. Although in point of fact the episode had stood her in good enough stead with the judges when it came to the separation.

But there you were. There was little to be gained by moping – not a hundred and seventy odd years later anyway. Alba or no Alba, life had been worth living. Failing the best, his heart had taught itself to alight on the nearest perch, and perches there had been aplenty. All he could do now, he supposed, was to chase the whole thing out of his system the way he had always done in the past, by jotting down a few verses about it, and then heigh ho! and on to think of something else.

For there were still things to think about, weren't there? That Anna creature, for example, who he had spoken with recently – the pretty, gentle-sounding one who had some breeding about her. She was the only one of his questioners to date who had managed to arouse his curiosity a little. He could think of her for a start. In fact he might even entitle the verses he was about to write 'To A——a', and see if they wouldn't do double duty: put his mind to rest about Alba and get him off to a good start with this other young woman. Hmm. Good idea. Now for the rhymes.

'Christ Almighty look at that! It's spouted!'
   'So it has! So it has!'
   'It's done it!'
   'Socks to the Haiku people! What's a miserable three lines compared to this?'
   'Here's to LB!'
   'Here's to LA. What a showing we'll make.'
   'Congratulations! I take back what I said about the parameters.'
   'Congratulations! I take back what I said about the grasshoppers. I've an idea we may really be on the right track at last. Twelve lines, all scanning. What more could anyone want?'
   'What a turn-up for the books!'
   'What a flower in our buttonhole!'
   'What a breakthrough!'
   'What a coup!'
   All argument temporarily forgotten, the Professor and his two assistants were standing clinking glasses over the terminal, and as they clinked they spilled yet more wine — a certain amount of which landed not on the terminal this time but on Anna's hair.
   'Ah Anna,' said the Professor, looking downwards and remembering to include her in the general jubilation, 'wonderful work, wonderful work. I think we'll have to ask permission from your University to take you to America with us. It looks as if you're the only one of us who can really get LB to do his stuff.'
   The proposal made Anna feel rather happy of a sudden. Although why the prospect of spending yet another week in the company of these three not parti-

172

cularly nice people should be so welcome to her, she did not really know. 'I'm on leave now for two weeks, she said quickly before the Professor could change his mind. 'I'd *love* to come. Thank you. There's nothing I'd like better.'

'Then that's settled,' said the Professor, who had in fact been about to retract the offer. 'We'll drink to it. Here's another glass of wine. Polish it off. And then if you don't mind, let's have the poem over again, right?'

Obligingly Anna downed the wine and then read the lines aloud a second time over in her best poetry voice.

'Pity it's such a bad poem,' commented the Professor with a laugh when the reading was over.

'Makes no odds,' said the male assistant, also laughing. 'Byron himself was a pretty bad poet.'

'Oh come now,' said his female counterpart. 'Over-rated perhaps, but not exactly *bad* surely.'

'But overrated as a lover, or so it seems,' chimed in the Professor, executing a few steps of Argentinian tango.

'Overrated as a lover.' 'Overrated as a poet.' 'Over-rated as a hero,' echoed the assistants.

'But *not*, fortunately for us,' pronounced the Professor triumphantly, swooping to sustain an imaginary partner in a back-bend, 'overrated as material for a computer program.'

It was too much for Anna to bear. Turning her back on them all and shutting her ears to their voices, she went back to the poem, and concentrated on a third reading.

I have followed your shadow (she read softly), *o'erstep-*
ping your shade,
I have lived, I have loved, that our love would ne'er fade;
And in places grown dark to me, calling your name,
I have courted your likeness, or ghosts of the same.

Your voice and your laugh and the curve of your breast
(The one place on earth where my heart has found rest),
I have sought them and found them and lost them apace;
And I'd lie if I said I'd no joy in the chase.

But believe me, if ever my words have been true,
In the images, traces, and mirrors of you,
In each heart I have plundered, each lip I have kissed,
It was you I was seeking and you that I missed.

'To A——a,' she mused. Augusta? Unlikely. Annabella? Impossible. To whom then? That was something she would have to think about. To her, anyway, it didn't seem a bad poem at all. On the contrary, she thought it was beautiful. Full of significance, if only she could work it out, and very, very moving.

Amanda Prantera was born in East Anglia and is a graduate of the University of London, where she read philosophy. She worked briefly as a translator and television writer before turning to full-time writing; she is the author of two novels, *Strange Loop* and *The Cabalist*. Amanda Prantera lives in Rome with her physician husband and two daughters.